Journeys into Staffordshire

Michael Pearson

hawksworth
graphics · print · sign

WAYZGOOSE

Published by Hawksworth
in association with Wayzgoose
Sladeside
Pennycroft Lane
Uttoxeter
Staffordshire
ST14 7QZ
Tel: 01889 565234
sales@hgandp.co.uk

ISBN 978-0-9562777-1-8

Contents

Preamble

Adolf Hitler, Doctor Beeching, Prime Minister Edward Heath – which is the odd man out?

I apologise: that was a trick question! There isn't an odd man out, all three of them did their best to undo the fabric of Britain in one way or another, and, if anything, Hitler had less far-reaching impact than the other two.

Beeching's activities are still notorious and continue to resonate in many towns and villages still disadvantaged by no longer being connected to the railway network. You will encounter him occasionally in these pages, for I find it impossible not to gnash my teeth when I come upon evidence of his ill-conceived axe; though, in retrospect, I can't help wondering if it wasn't Ernest Marples, the Conservative Minister for Transport, who encouraged him to destroy the railway network, that was the real villain. I don't believe that it was entirely coincidental that Marples owned a road-building business, and it says much about the character of the man that he also introduced yellow lines and postcodes.

But it was Edward Heath's government who pushed through the Local Government Act of 1972, altering county boundaries which in many cases could be traced back past the Norman Conquest to the Anglo Saxon shires and, as its figurehead, it is he who deserves the most disdain from traditionalists like me.

When the boundary changes took place in 1974, Staffordshire was robbed of a big chunk of the Black Country which had previously belonged to it. That chunk was absorbed into something unimaginatively known as the West Midlands. Hence, much to my disappointment – for I like nothing better than an industrial town – Wednesfield, Walsall and Wolverhampton, Brownhills, Bilston and West Bromwich could no longer be plausibly part of my peregrinations of Staffordshire.

Never mind, the rest of this unsung county lay waiting to be extolled. And to make things even more interesting, I decided to undertake my journeys of exploration by as many different means as I could conveniently muster. In itself, that added extra fun to the proceedings, but it also allowed for a range of different perspectives.

And what did I make of it, this 21st Century Staffordshire? Everywhere I went I seemed to have one foot in the past, though bear in mind that

Misty morning, Alton

Tight squeeze, Consall Forge

might say more about my own internal default setting than any shortcomings associated with the present. Entering Staffordshire by road one frequently has one's attention drawn to the fact that this is 'the creative county', though what form this creativity takes is not made clear: is it belated homage to Arnold Bennett; or Clarice Cliff; does it refer to the excitements of Alton Towers; or is it an oblique tribute to the county council's accountants?

It was educational to discover just how many different Staffordshires there really are: from the flatlands bordering the Trent and the Tame to the wild hill country around Longnor; from the breweries of Burton to the potteries of Stoke; from the heights of Kinver Edge to the remote farmlands bordering Shropshire. It tickled me·that there appeared to be no *West* Staffordshire, not in common parlance at any rate, let alone a local authority portfolio of hospitals, libraries and road gritters as assembled under the banners of North, South and East Staffordshire.

Were there highlights? Hundreds of them, and you will need to read the full text to find them; no 'box outs' or easily assimilated bullet points to help you here! Were there disappointments? Not many, but I wish the Staffordshire Way was better maintained and better advertised, though those two concerns may not be entirely unconnected. It is not particularly a problem solely encountered

in Staffordshire, but I would advocate urgent rationalisation of the burgeoning plethora of signage which afflicts one at almost every turn. I would try to do something about on-street parking too. In many cases it is practically impossible to photograph street scenes effectively due to the sheer ugliness of the assembled lines of modern vehicles. Imagine how much lovelier the thoroughfares of our towns and villages would be without them. Oh, and don't even get me started on street lights!

And did I miss anything? Mountains of stuff, I could have filled four books. And, even as we went to press, fresh nuggets of intriguing information jostled for inclusion: how Captain Smith of Titanic infamy came to be remembered in a statue in a Lichfield park sculpted by Scott of Antarctica's widow; Hednesford's Gaskin murder of 1919; Hanley's abandoned Post Office built of Alton stone; the rocky promontories offering an eagle's eye view of the Churnet Valley that I somehow missed at Toothill. I'll just have to go back and follow in my own footsteps, as I hope that you will too. It would be nice if we all rediscovered our counties, both topographically – as in the following pages – but also in the sense that we take a reinvigorated delight in belonging to them. Without noticing it, we have all become council tax debtors belonging to one local authority or another. It's high time we became proud natives of a *county* again.

Lichfield Cathedral: West view; East view; Stowe Pool

Soft Pedalling

IS there anywhere on earth as heavenly as an English cathedral close? If the one at Lichfield was anything to go by that bright June morning, the answer is incontrovertibly no.

In their pristine black and yellow blazers, and equally commendable deportment, pupils from the Cathedral School were filing through the North Door for a service. The organ was audibly welling up to some hymnal climax as I pedalled away, but I was humming a different tune, for National Cycle Route 54 had reminded my convoluted thought processes of Chuck Berry and *Route 66*. Route 54 runs all the way from Stourport-on-Severn to Derby, but I wasn't going to follow it very far, it would just be my escape clause from the city's suburbs.

I rode beside Stowe Pool, celebrated (locally, at least) for its crayfish, its carp and its abundance of water lilies, then on past some allotments, before reaching the ring-road where a modern pub called the Dr Johnson was being advertised for sale. I wondered what withering comment the great 18th Century wit would have to utter about that. The West Coast Main Line railway appears, for the time being at any rate, to have prevented any further expansion of Lichfield's suburbs. Once across it, I was out into open countryside and listening to birdsong as opposed to the roar of traffic: it was like exchanging Status Quo for Schubert, and I was pleased with the transaction.

The lane zigzagged through yellow fields of rape. I braked to allow a young blonde to cross in front of me, leading a piebald horse from its stable to a field, and noted a striking similarity in the arrangement of their pony-tails. Next I passed the entrance to Curborough Sprint Course. Racing cars, motorcycles and bicycles have been put through their paces here since 1963, but I was tickled to discover that the course's main claim to fame is that it features in the *Guinness Book of Records* as the venue for a thousand mile pedal car race in 2002.

The sprint course was fashioned out of land previously occupied by a Second World War aerodrome, RAF Lichfield. A little further on I encountered evidence of its former existence in the shape of a 'blister' shaped hangar, now used as a warehouse on what has become a busy industrial estate. A handful of these hangars remain, redolent

of a different age and purpose. A far cry from 30th May 1942 when the station took part in Bomber Harris's infamous thousand bomber raid on Cologne. Twenty-one Wellingtons took off from Lichfield on the mission, and thankfully none were shot down. Later in the war the aerodrome was used as a postal sorting centre by the Americans, and afterwards it was used for dispersals and storage. At one time over fifteen hundred aircraft being assembled here before it finally closed in 1958. Legend has it that a headless figure in flying kit haunts the site now. All I could see was a huge new Tesco warehouse with an elephantine queue of juggernauts assembled outside, waiting to unload their contents. Ah, the dividends of peace!

I cycled on. Summer marched beside me. In the verge Jack by the hedge had all but gone and nettles were beginning to suffocate the cow parsley. High above, a buzzard was being harried by a pair of crows. The image brought to mind a bomber being intercepted by fighter planes.

A bridge with a pronounced hump led me over the Coventry Canal and, leaving Route 54, I carried my bicycle down some steps to join the towpath just as a boat called *Tuppence* chugged through the arch. Canal boats are limited to four miles an hour – no wonder it's perceived as such a good way of slowing down – and I soon left them astern. Furthermore *Tuppence's* crew would have to operate a swing-bridge to reach Fradley Junction and I wouldn't!

Isolated meeting place of the Coventry and Trent & Mersey canals, I've known Fradley Junction for forty years, and I know which one of us has changed more: Fradley has mellowed with age, and I'm not sure that I have. On account of the Swan Inn it has always been popular, but nowadays there are a couple of cafés too, together with an information centre based at British Waterways maintenance depot, a picturesque conglomeration of workshops and outbuildings dating back to the early days of the Trent & Mersey Canal. The canal and its locks are not the only water feature either, for a small reservoir, attractively cupped in woodland, has been opened out in recent years, and there's a hide where you can go to watch the local birdlife.

A bright red boat was negotiating Keeper's Lock

as I mounted my bicycle once more and pedalled off in the direction of Fradley village, encountering Route 54 again in the process, but not being tempted to follow it directly to Alrewas because I hankered after exploring the isolated tract of land which lies east of the A38.

New housing has seen Fradley expand in recent years, but it still has a quaint little chapel-like church called St Stephens, and I paused to take a photograph of its charming doorway which bears the advice of King Solomon: 'KEEP THY FOOT WHEN THOU GOEST TO THE HOUSE OF GOD'. A flyover carried me safely across the A38. I was not envious of the hurrying motorists below.

Then commenced a strange interlude as I embarked on a ride through a curiously remote parcel of countryside, well off the beaten track, between the A38 and the River Tame. It seemed appropriate that I should have to pass through a gate to reach this forgotten world. It may have been merely a railway level-crossing to some unromantic observers, an irritating obstacle in their mad dash to their next appointment, but to me it had all the intrigue of a border post. In fact I was rather sorry that I didn't have a car with me, because had I done so, the attendant would have had to come out of his cabin and open the wider of the two pairs of timber gates for my benefit. As it was he was able to call a cheery greeting and tell me that the line was clear for me to push my way through the narrower pedestrian gates. I rather envied him his idyllic occupation. Along the tracks, in the direction of Lichfield, a little knot of day-glo coloured track-workers shimmered in the heat.

Beyond the level-crossing the landscape lay Fenland-like in its flatness. The fields either side of me were given over to barley and wheat. A few early foxgloves sprouted from neighbouring ditches. A sign proclaimed that the road ahead was 'unsuitable for motors', I can confirm that it was hardly suitable for bicycles either. I passed a fellow cyclist gingerly proceeding in the opposite direction. 'Bumpy isn't it!' he observed. 'Y-y-you can-n-n s-s-say that-t-t ag-g-gain,' I joked, but he was downwind and already out of earshot-t-t.

An equally bumpy mode of transport, in the shape of a microlight, was taking off from a neighbouring field, its occupant had chosen a fine day for his flight. At Whitemoor Haye an abandoned farmhouse presented a melancholy sight. 'Haye' is the old Saxon word for a hunting park. Nowadays they hunt here for gravel, not game. Some of the abandoned workings were being used unsavourily as a landfill site. The lane rose briefly to cross a conveyor belt.

The National Memorial Arboretum has come a long way in a short time. By the time its woodland has fully matured it will be a very special place indeed. And its location, between two railway lines and between two rivers, cuts it off nicely from the outside world, lending it just the right level of quietude

Fradley Junction

for introspection and reflection. To do it full justice you need more time than I had at my disposal – the quick and the dead it commemorates deserve all the time you can give them. But I was determined, at least, to follow the pathways which wend their way through the arboretum to see the confluence of the rivers Trent and Tame. Out of respect I abandoned my bicycle at the cycle park and set out on foot, though when I saw that the centre now boasted a 'road train' I did have second thoughts.

In the business of remembering man's inhumanity to man, less – I always find – is more. A simple plaque on a tree commemorating a single individual is equally as poignant as a huge installation such as the centre's dominant feature, the Armed Forces Memorial, which remembers those who have died in conflict since the end of the Second World War.

I progressed via various pathways to the far end of the arboretum where it peters out almost imperceptibly in thistly meadows where the Tame gives itself up to the Trent. This fluvial sacrifice sort of echoes all the other sacrifices recalled throughout the arboretum. I paused for a moment or two to think about that, before a train rushed by on its way towards Birmingham and broke the spell, and I wondered how many of its passengers had any idea as to the nature and purpose of the site they were hurrying through. Perhaps the trains should be made to stop for a minute out of respect.

On my way back I came upon an old Second World War pill box on the banks of the Tame. This was no commemorative 'installation', but rather a

Armed Forces Memorial

Shot at Dawn

genune survivor from a time when there was a real fear that we might be invaded. You encounter them from time to time still littering the banks of rivers and canals, because it was always felt that waterways could be strategic lines of defence. It seemed appropriate that it was still here, and a metaphor for enduring peace that visitors were encouraged to use it as a bird hide.

The old Croxall road into Alrewas doesn't get there anymore, on account of the A38's dual-carriageway. They had to demolish an inn called the Paul Pry when the road was widened in the early 1960s. If you're a pedestrian or a cyclist you can use this quieter approach, and in doing so are treated to another level crossing, this one without timber gates alas, but a handsome signal box more than makes up for the automatic barriers in use now. Alrewas's station stood here until Beechinged out of existence in 1965. One imagines it would be a useful commuter railhead now if whoever's currently in charge of the destiny of our railway network ever get around to reopening it.

You can take your chances crossing the road, or you can essay a half mile detour via the nearest overbridge to the south. With an unwieldy bicycle to contend with, I sensibly selected the latter option. Alrewas, like Fradley, has grown a good deal over the years. But, pedalling along Main Street, I could decipher the older properties, and picture how the village must have looked in earlier days. Some of them are thatched and timber-framed and date back as far as the 16th and 17th centuries.

The name Alrewas (pronounced in such a way as to rhyme with 'walrus') is said to derive from Alderwasse, old English for alder tree and marsh. But the settlement probably goes back much further than that, after all, the Roman road known as Ryknild Street ran right past it – a shame that it's now known much less romantically as the A38!

Once upon a time, basket-weaving was Alrewas's stock in trade, but now – as if to emphasise the suburbanisation of the village – I found myself cycling past a fish & chip shop, a Chinese take-away and a Co-op: good practical facilities, no doubt, but much more picturesque are the premises of Peter Coates, a butcher who specialises in high quality, locally reared meats. With racks of vegetables and sacks of potatoes stacked beneath its awning, and a mouth-watering array of meats visible through the doorway, it was difficult to resist not stopping for at least a hand-raised pork pie. In fact a bit of an argument broke out between me and my conscience, and he – dull fellow that he is – won.

Trying not to sulk, I bore right at the War Memorial and turned into Post Office Road at the far end of which – if you know where to look – you can spot a comical error dating from the coronation of George V. Perhaps it took the news that there was a new monarch on the throne some

The Trent at Alrewas

time to reach Alrewas, because its Coronation Square is dated 1911, the following year. Perhaps the excitement was too much for the man responsible for carving its name plate, perhaps he'd lunched too well at The Crown across the road. Look closely and you'll see that he spelt it 'Coronatation Square'! I was glad the error had survived in perpetuity, though oddly I don't feel the same way about the spelling mistakes in some of the books I've written.

Somewhat sadly – if not inevitably – Alrewas Mill – once a flourishing regional manufacturer of animal feeds with its own distinctive fleet of delivery lorries – has been converted into flats. I wondered at what point posterity would wake up to the error of abandoning manufacturing as a means of amassing wealth in favour of property development. I liked the story about the mill concerning its name being painted in large, proud letters on the roof, and how it had to be removed when the Second World War broke out lest enemy aviators used it to identify their location.

Next it was back to the Trent & Mersey Canal, which winds through the village on its way between Fradley Junction and Burton-on-Trent. Below Alrewas Lock – which was occupied by a jaunty little cabin cruiser as I passed – the canal is joined by a sudden visitor in the shape of the River Trent. This is an unusual, though not unique, arrangement dating back to the construction of the canal by James Brindley in the last quarter of the 18th Century. He may have been looking to bolster water supplies – one of the biggest problems facing any canal builder – or something in the flat and marshy nature of the surrounds may have precluded the construction of an aqueduct. Whatever Brindley's thinking, the short union between natural and man-made waterways means that in times of flood after heavy rainfall, the canal has to be temporarily closed to boat traffic, otherwise steerers might find themselves disappearing rather too rapidly for their liking over the nearby weir.

There was no such commotion on the day I was there. The river's current was barely detectable and the water was so clear that I could make out differing kinds of weed in its bed. I waited some time for Ophelia to float along, to no avail. I cycled over a sequence of metal footbridges which must presumably have been provided to keep the hooves of the horses who towed the boats dry when the meadows were in flood. This is a particularly pretty stretch of canal, almost ethereal in its reed-fringed isolation. On the opposite bank some cattle were cooling-off, knee-deep in the water's margin. In contrast, a narrow boat had moored up against one

Barton-under-Needwood

of the footbridges and its occupants were sunbathing in alarming degrees of nakedness on the roof.

Perched on a hillside above the canal, the little brick-towered church at Wychnor came into view. I left the towpath here, heaving my bicycle up shoulder high to negotiate a stile. A man in sartorially-challenged shorts walked past me singing aloud; another man in a hard hat was scything the grass in the churchyard; a young woman came down the lane on a horse: forget wilderness, Wychnor was positively crowded!

Crossing the lane which leads to Wychnor Park, I rejoined National Cycle Route 54 for an enjoyable journey along a green lane to Barton-under-Needwood. My tyres swished, insects droned, a gentle breeze cooled my forehead; from the giant eyesore of the Argos warehouse on the horizon, I averted my gaze.

Staffordshire place names don't come much more mellifluous than Barton-under-Needwood, yet the village itself is a bit too built-up to satisfy the average traveller's urge for the picturesque. Even Barton Green belies its name, consisting largely of bungalows. The Royal Oak looked congenial enough, but it was not yet noon and opening time. Route 54 led me past the 16th Century church, given to the village by its most famous son, John

St Mary's, Dunstall

Taylor, a triplet who went on to become Master of the Rolls in the reign of Henry VIII. In the shadow of the imposing old vicarage, a well-preserved Staffordshire County Council signpost pointed resolutely, if somewhat inaccurately now, to Barton & Walton railway station, closed down in 1958! Pupils were pouring out of the John Taylor School, presumably for their lunches. This is perhaps not the place to remark that they looked less well-attired, though not necessarily less well-educated, than their contemporaries at Lichfield Cathedral School.

Pigs were frolicking in woods on the outskirts of the village. I left the well-signposted cycle route at Dunstall, an estate village of considerable charm, well known locally for its cricket club. The church, with its tall landmark of a spire, is of Victorian origin. In recent times the imposing hall (now used as an events venue, but once owned by the Arkwrights) has been variously owned by individuals who made their fortunes in gravel extraction and property development: fortunately for them, they did not need to live 'over the shop'. Dunstall's enduring joke concerns the nature of the White Lion, not a pub as visitors were led to suppose, but a roadside well. It's still there, though not available for refreshment of any sort.

So far my journey had been largely free of inclines. Now I was climbing up into the purlieus of the old Needwood Forest, once one of England's most extensive areas of woodland, a triangular plateau rising to over four hundred feet above sea level, bounded on two sides by the Trent and on the other by the Dove. At its greatest extent the forest amounted to some nine thousand acres of woodland, but this was significantly reduced by the enclosures which took place at the beginning of the 19th Century. There were eco-warriors even then. Poetry was written in protest. Francis Noel Clarke Mundy – one of the Mundys of Markeaton, Derby – published an anthology entitled Needwood Forest that included contributions from Erasmus Darwin and the Lichfield poetess, Anna Seward. The artist, Joseph Wright of Derby, painted a pastoral scene depicting a cottage in the heart of the forest. To no avail. Progress marched, as it always does, blithely on.

Needwood remains idyllic, though barely five hundred acres of woodland now exist, and this is being subsumed within the new National Forest, of which it forms the western third. The National Forest embraces two hundred square miles and its promoters aspire to approximately a third of that area being covered in trees. Seven million trees have already been planted, many in districts of neighbouring Derbyshire and Leicestershire formerly occupied by heavy industry. All very laudable, but am I alone in feeling that the name might have been less bland or vague? National in the context of three midland counties seems positively misleading. And already I have witnessed regrettable examples of tree planting. Where once the

Meynell Ingram Arms

Needwood escarpment rose like a sensuously bare downland ridge out of the Trent Valley in the vicinity of Tatenhill, now it is ubiquitously wooded.

I came to a series of switchback gradients known as Scotch Hills. Happily the descents were so steep that I gathered sufficient momentum to ascend the ensuing gradients with just enough puff to spare me the embarrassment of getting off and pushing. Crossing the A515 Lichfield to Ashbourne main road at Newchurch, I found myself descending through a belt of remaining woodland into the scattered village of Hoar Cross and the welcoming embrace of the Meynell Ingram Arms.

In my youth The Meynell had a reputation for being awfully posh, if not downright condescending. Having changed hands a number of times in recent years, I sensed a more egalitarian approach as I entered the bar: certainly the welcome was not as refreshingly cool as the beer. Overcoming my initial disappointment that locally brewed Blythe Bitter was not on tap, I ordered a pint of beer called Merchant Navy which hailed from Somerset. It may regrettably have left its carbon footprint all the way up the M5, but I can vouch for its efficacy and, having arrived on two wheels rather than four, I ordered another to accompany a ham sandwich which in no time at all was brought to me in the garden by a pretty young blonde.

Watered and fuelled, I went up the next hill like one of the steam locomotives that the beer had been named after. Luckily, after the lung-bursting effort involved, I didn't have far to go to my next venue, George Frederick Bodley's extraordinary Church of the Holy Angels. In Betjeman's opinion it was Bodley's masterpiece. Embowered as it is on three sides, the sheer size of the church does not hit you at first. Why so big? There was surely never the population to make up the sort of congregational numbers its great nave could cater for. To echo Todd Rundgren's song: *Love is the Answer*. The love of Emily Meynell-Ingram for her lately departed husband Hugo. She caused it to be erected in his memory. Work commenced in 1872, and four years later this great Gothic Revival edifice was dedicated, though – as if it wasn't already large enough – additions were still being built on as late as 1906.

More subfusc than the village pub, the interior took some getting accustomed to, but little by little my eyes began to appreciate the grandeur and the detail. In a perhaps untypical act of piety, I made it my business to follow the Stations of the Cross, down the west wall and up the east, marvelling at the intricacy of the Flemish carvings, and not unmoved by, or immune to, the unfolding drama.

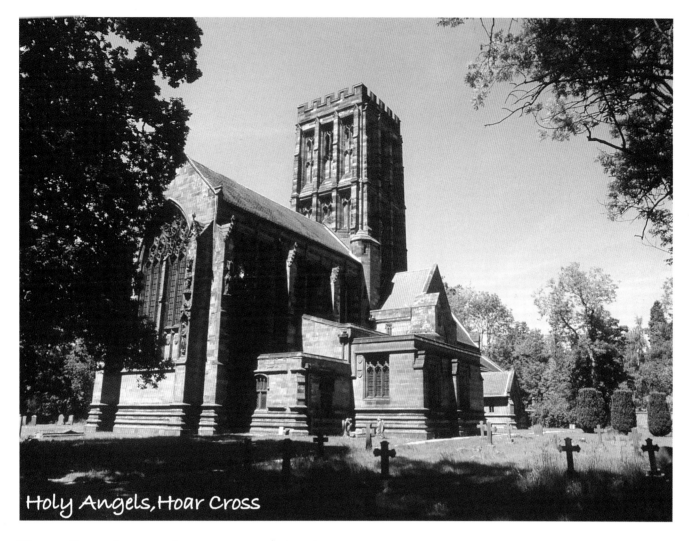

Holy Angels, Hoar Cross

Then a disappointment: the nave was open but the chancel was not. My way barred beyond the rood screen, I was unable to approach Meynell-Ingram's tombs, nor stare up from below into the hollow infinity of the tower, where, who knows, possibly heaven waited. Thus symbolically abandoned in limbo, I retreated to the familiarity of the secular world outside, no longer potentially a pilgrim, merely a tourist.

The Meynell-Ingram's pile, Hoar Cross Hall, is more plebeian than plutocratic now, having flung its doors open to the *hoi polloi* in the guise of a 'Spa Resort'. Resisting blandishments to 'revitalise and de-stress', I pedalled past its gates, preferring the call of the open road where my fitness regime was concerned. Thorney Lanes carried me along a contour which runs, south to north, with the grain of the countryside. Roost Hill and Dark Lane elected to plunge down into the neighbouring valley, but I kept to the high ground. By Pound Farm I crossed the B5234. At Holt Hill Farm they were busy silaging and cattle were sensibly gathered under the shade of an oak. At Buttermilk Hill I followed their wise example and threw myself down in the long grass to study the map. It was an apposite place to pause. Ahead of me the road was about to leap off the

edge of the escarpment, my sojourn in Needwood Forest was coming to an end.

It's not exactly that I would advocate *not* using the brakes in the descent of Buttermilk Hill, though nevertheless it is exhilarating not to do so. Had it not been for Gorsty Hill I may have broken the sound barrier as well as every bone in my body. Dogs barked at me at Scounslow Green. Given my yellow top, it was perhaps inevitable that they should mistake me for Lance Armstrong. A little further on the road crossed the Staffordshire Way making its way across farmland between Uttoxeter and Abbots Bromley. Looking forward to doing that walk at a later date, I crossed the B5013 at crossroads once presided over by an inn called the Red Cow. It is now merely a private home, the fate of many a public house unless, that is, they have been enterprisingly transformed into an Indian restaurant.

Loxley Green came and went without troubling my notepad or my pen. It is astonishing how quickly you can lose yourself in this empty corner of the Staffordshire countryside. Not cartographically lost, that is, but lost in the sense that there is nothing to hold on to; no landmarks, no lifebelt so to speak. A man was driving away from Manor Golf Club with a smile on his face. I imagined he'd sunk a cheeky

putt on the seventeenth, and that his opponent had not had time to get back on level terms.

At Aldery Bank I turned left onto the Stafford road, and was about to let go of the brakes when I spotted the elegiac inscription 'dismtd rly' on the map and the symbolic suggestion of a cutting leading to a tunnel. Of course I was well aware that this was the old Stafford & Uttoxeter Railway, an outpost, no less of the mighty London & North Eastern empire. A farm track running parallel proved too tempting to the ferroequinologist in me. I free-wheeled a few yards down it and found a gap in what had long ago been the railway company's wire and concrete fence. In winter it would have been a much easier proposition. In summer, in shorts, I was nettle fodder.

Painstakingly I made my way down through this stinging undergrowth to the former trackbed. Presumably time had taken its toll of the railway builder's drainage arrangements. Tentatively I forged ahead through what was now a passable imitation of a swamp. Oddly enough the fallen trees, frequent as they were, came to my rescue, enabling me to surmount a number of boggy bits that would otherwise have defeated me. But in the end I came to a halt perhaps ten yards from the perfectly preserved tunnel mouth. By then I'd been outmanoeuvred half way up the side of the cutting and the ground beneath my feet was just too precarious to proceed. Passenger trains stopped

using the line at the outbreak of the Second World War, and goods not long after hostilities ceased. But the southern portal of what was known as Bromshall Tunnel (a railway corruption of Bramshall!) enigmatically stood its ground, dreaming of the days when overnight milk trains puffed through it, carrying the creamy output of the Trent Valley's contented cows to the breakfast tables of London.

The River Blithe has its source on high ground to the east of Stoke-on-Trent and preserves its independence for some twenty, largely undemonstrative miles before being consumed by the Trent in the vicinity of Kings Bromley. We will meet it again when it makes its one big gesture at Blithfield Reservoir. Where the river is crossed by the A518, there is a picturesque watermill. Not a fully functioning watermill, naturally – they are few and far between these days – but one that has been adapted for domestic use. Better than demolition – it would be difficult to argue otherwise – but still a tantalisingly pale shadow of its past, rather like the dismantled railway I'd just encountered. The Uttoxeter to Stafford road is not for those of a nervous disposition, nor for dreamy travel writers prone to stop without officially sanctioned signals for the purposes of note taking and/or photography. So I was glad to turn aside and follow a winding by-road languorously up the valley while I still had all my limbs.

In due course I came to Gratwich, indolent

under the blazing sun. I turned aside to see the church and was not disappointed. The afternoon heat had relinquished the pleasing aroma of creosote from the churchyard's pair of timber gates. I walked between gravestones all but masked by high waving grasses, trusting that the occupants preferred that more natural arrangement to a municipally pristine sward. The diminutive church itself was self-effacingly built of brick, a bell-cote its sole ostentation. One can seldom tell, until the knob is turned – more in hope than expectation – whether ingress will be forthcoming. The size or location of the church rarely appears to play any part in this game of chance. Eloquent in its emptiness, the interior moved me in quite differently a way to Hoar Cross. God was here too, and had simply taken a short-cut; either that, or he had cycled determinedly by while I was gazing into the portal of Bromshall Tunnel.

On the outskirts of Gratwich I had to pull into a field entry to let a feedstuffs lorry overtake me. In doing so I was rewarded with a panoramic vista of the Blithe Valley with what I took to be Church Leigh prominent in the distance. Only when it occurred to me that I had to cycle all that way, did the view pall somewhat.

Briefly I joined the B5027, the road which links Uttoxeter with Stone. I crossed the Blithe and entered a place imaginatively known as Field. A Victorian post box caught my eye, underlying just how off the beaten track I was. Further nostalgia was forthcoming in the barns of Field Farm, within which I spied an array of vintage buses, not least a Gash of Newark double-decker.

Along a lane upon which grass grew down the middle like a Mohican hair cut, I reeled off those intimidating miles to Church Leigh. At Bents Bridges I crossed the North Staffordshire Railway's Stoke to Derby line, leaning over the parapet to see the double track curving sinuously beneath. Council houses formed a nondescript introduction to Church Leigh. Bland new-builds preceded a curiously imposing church, steadfastly locked: as was a pub called The Star. Whatever went on in the village it didn't happen in the middle of the afternoon. Or did it? – Behind closed doors! I rode on, passing beneath the A50, a concrete road I've noisily and indifferently hurtled along more times than I care to remember.

With the innate superiority of one who is self-propelled, I dropped down the steep and sinuous incline to Lower Tean, crossing its eponymous river in the process. The Tean is a tributary of the Dove. Innocuous enough it looks now, but once it powered the tape mills of Upper Tean, in the direction of which I was soon pedalling assiduously along the A522. First, though, I couldn't help noticing the unusually handsome buildings of Heybridge Farm. Delving later into the history of the neighbourhood, I discovered that its had been the home farm for a big house called The Heybridge which had been built by a branch of the Philips family who had developed the mills in Upper Tean. Unfortunately

Soft Pedalling into Lower Tean

the house was demolished in the 1950s. If its model farm was anything to go by, it must have been an impressive building.

* * *

Nine days had passed since the weather was good enough to allow me to continue my ride – flaming June, and yes, the adjective is pejorative! In fact it didn't look all that convincing at Upper Tean; blustery with scudding clouds. But the weather forecasters said it would remain dry, and I had fallen into the usual trap of trusting them.

Upper Tean is dominated by its textile mills, even though now they are not in the business of making tape anymore but housing people. The Philips brothers began weaving here in the middle of the 18th Century, adapting half-timbered Tean Hall of 1613 as their headquarters. It still stands, annexed to a handsome Georgian building once used as the mill manager's house: how seamlessly the architecture melds, would that that were so of the new-builds recently erected to the rear. Three huge multi-storey mills were built in the 19th Century, the last to be erected, in 1885, overlooking the main street. The Philips family were altruistic employers. Mothers were encouraged to return to work as soon as possible after childbirth. Nurses cared for the infants, but the mothers were on hand to breast feed. Altruistic? – Or perhaps just shrewd, I'll let you decide!

From the profits the Philips purchased the Heath estate on the neighbouring hillside (above the pall of chimney smoke?) and transformed it into a Gothic pile. It's still up there and still in the family, who market it now as a centre for events, weddings, functions and filming. In recent years television

Croft Mill Chimney, Upper Tean

versions of *The Hound of the Baskervilles* and *Miss Marple* have used its brooding atmospheric setting for dastardly deeds.

Back down in Tean, the mills churned out tape for two centuries before succumbing, one presumes, to competition from the Far East. During the Second World War they produced material for parachutes, name tags for undercover agents, and medal ribbons. I wondered if the new denizens would ever know such purpose, such excitement, but somehow doubted it: a new sofa from MFI would be about the sum total of their ambitions.

A milestone tucked into the wall outside a hairdressing salon informed me that I was 146 miles from London and 65 miles from Liverpool. Its relevance must date back to the days when this was the A50, a trunk road running all the way from Northampton to Warrington. Now, of course, the bulk of the traffic keeps to the dual-carriagewayed A50 which by-passes Tean, but there still appeared to be traffic enough on the road to Cheadle as I set off in that direction, with one eye cocked suspiciously towards those clouds.

Squat mill-worker terraces gave way to angular bay-windowed semis as the outskirts were negotiated. A lofty factory chimney recalled another element of Tean's industrial past. Now it looked like an exclamation mark, perhaps relating to a joke or a shock. Whichever, it seemed reconciled that smoke no longer billowed from its tip. Subsequently I discovered from an old map that it had been part of Croft Mill, a bleach and dye works.

A plethora of roadside pubs illustrated the need

The Market, Cheadle

place.

But before religion and architecture I needed sustenance and, this being North Staffordshire, sought it at Ye Olde Oatcake Shoppe. There was a bit of a queue and it didn't thin very quickly. Oatcakes are a serious proposition, rather like communion it occurred to me. While I was waiting I read a newspaper cutting that had been sellotaped up on the wall. It informed me that the Shoppe's owner was Malcolm Tellwright, a good old Potteries name if ever there was one. Had we been on our own I might have jokingly asked if he was descended from Anna of the Five Towns.

Malcolm, it transpired, had had the business handed down to him by an uncle, and with the business the secret recipe! I know a bit about the cloak and dagger world of oatcake making. I know that all the proprietors of these undertakings pride themselves that their ingredients are superior to those of their rivals. The newspaper article claimed that Malcolm was scornful of keeping his recipe in a safe. It was securer, he insisted, in his head. 'Only torture, or loads o' money could make me reveal it,' he'd quipped. One look at him convinced me that neither was likely to prise the secret from his lips. Being mid-morning, I contented myself with just the one oatcake.

to slake industrial-sized thirsts, a number of them having post-industrially lost the will to live and gone to that great licensed victuallers association in the sky. The road plunged through a rocky cutting festooned in ferns. Signposts to the quarries at Croxden and Freehay explained the preponderance of motorway maintenance lorries. Another road sign, pointing in the direction of Winnothdale, gave me my first redolent whiff of The North.

Head bent over the handlebars, I looked up and beheld a sign which read: 'Welcome to Cheadle – Historic Market Town'. 'Ah, if only I'd had a pound for every municipally ordained 'historic market town' I had entered,' I sighed.

It didn't appear very historic to begin with: bungalows and bus stops, an estate pub and a Spar convenience store seemed all too mundane and modern to me. But as I progressed there were mitigating interludes: a cricket club and a re-creation ground; and an unsolicited greeting from a little man carrying a large shopping bag. Crueller, more worldly correspondents might have used the term 'midget', I was simply touched. And then I saw the upturned, pencil-thin spire of St Giles and remembered why I had included the pigeon-fancying town of Cheadle in my itinerary in the first

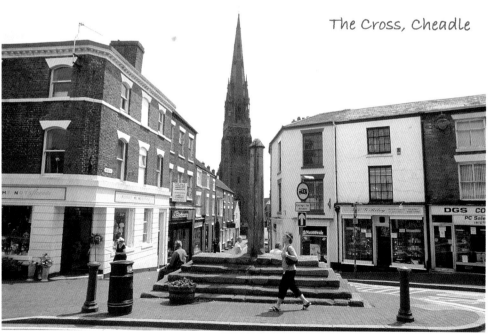

The Cross, Cheadle

From the mouthwatering list of possible fillings I selected a gastronomic combination of bacon, cheese and mushrooms and went down Cross Street chewing contentedly.

Is it possible to encounter two ecclesiastical masterpieces on one bike ride? Seemingly so, for if Hoar Cross is considered Bodley's best church, St Giles at Cheadle is usually quoted as Pugin's. Both owe a great debt to the Gothic Revival. And if Hoar Cross is high - in both senses of the term - Cheadle is Roman Catholic to its core. A frail lady was taking her leave as I pushed through the door.

'Oh, I've just put the lights out,' she told me with an apologetic air. 'You'll need to put a pound in the slot.'

'Will I need light?' I asked, wondering if she would mistake this for a theological enquiry.

'Oh, to do it justice, yes!' she exclaimed enthusiastically.

For a pound I got fifteen minutes of light. The guide cost another three pounds, and I gave a pound to the donation box designated: 'For the Poor', looking to see if there were any claim forms handy. The thorough guide book encouraged me to perambulate clockwise. There was the faintest whiff of incense: it took me, kicking and screaming, back to my convent education. As guided, I went and stood below the tower arch to appreciate the interior as a whole. It struck me that not a square inch of surface remained undecorated. If the Good Lord had a weakness for Laura Ashley then he would undoubtedly feel at home here.

The uninitiated will be asking themselves why such a jewel dwells in an unfashionable town like Cheadle. The answer lies in the Catholic Emancipation Act of 1829 and the determination of the Earl of Shrewsbury at nearby Alton Towers to spare no expense in the erection of a Catholic church in his nearest town. And having worked on the Earl's estate at Alton, and being a fanatical convert to Catholicism himself, Augustus Welby Northmore Pugin was, in the contemporary jargon, a shoo-in for the job. Posterity has applauded the Earl's gesture, even if he must have blanched at seeing the bill rise eightfold from an initial estimate of five thousand pounds.

I think the Lady Chapel was my favourite, in particular a triptych altar-piece depicting the Passion of Christ. Both Pugin and Lord Shrewsbury were apparently avid collectors of medieval ecclesiastical art and this intricate woodcarving is 15th Century Flemish. In the Chapel of Blessed Sacrament an A4 photocopy requested prayer 'for the souls who have died this year'. 'Died', I repeated to myself: 'Don't

St Giles, Cheadle

souls live on?'

The Visitor's Book contained addresses from all over the world, together with enthusiastic epithets such as 'fabulous', 'extraordinary', 'remarkable' and 'wondrous'. One lady called Marion had made a Puginesque pilgrimage all the way from the Landmark Trust's self-catering accommodation at Alton Station on foot. When the time came to write my comments I was tempted to put: 'a bit overpowering on top of an oatcake', but then a church as fine as St Giles' is no place to give in to temptation, is it?

Secular Cheadle is not without a certain appeal of its own. With more time at my disposal I might have happily patronised the Tudor Tea Room. I liked the look of the Market Square too, admiring its Georgian buildings, notwithstanding brash 'To Let' signs disfiguring their façade. Unsure as to when refreshments would next be forthcoming, I called in at a sandwich bar for a coffee. The women behind the counter were saying something about 'running'. I pricked up my ears and said:

'Running?'

'She's my trainer,' laughed the one who was serving me. 'I'm getting ready to do the Great North Run. I'm being sponsored for Cancer Research.'

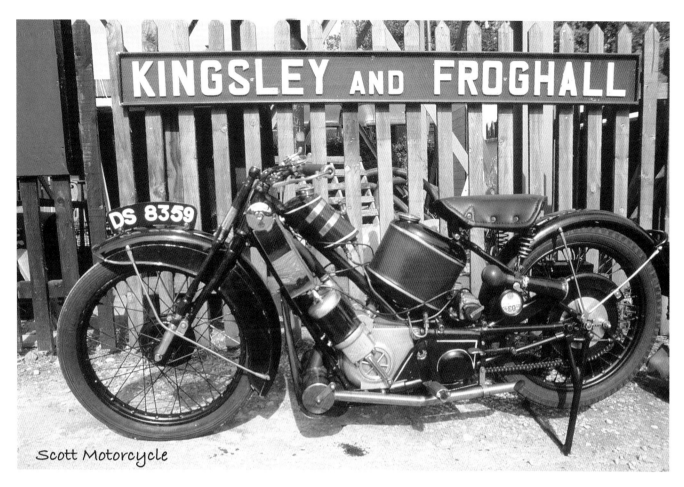

Scott Motorcycle

'And have you done a half-marathon before?' I asked, politely not referring directly to her girth.

'Not me,' she giggled.

'I've got her up to five miles,' added her trainer optimistically.

'Well here's a pound towards your sponsorship,' I said.

'Ooh thanks,' said the prospective runner. 'At least I know I've got the first mile sponsored.'

'Oh no,' I said, taking my coffee and backing out through the door, 'that's for the last mile!'

Freewheeling out of town, I wasn't fooled, wave upon wave of moorland gradients stretched ahead. Neither was I fooled by the sign which offered 'an ideal business opportunity' to anyone gullible enough to take on the tenancy of The Miners Rest, a boarded-up pub on the edge of town. It gave every indication of being as impossible to resurrect as the local industry which had once inspired its name.

There was a time when Cheadle stood at the epicentre of its own coalfield. From reference material in the local studies section of Cheadle Library I drew the conclusion that the Miner's Rest had probably been associated with Woodhead Colliery which had stood to the east of the Cheadle to Froghall turnpike. The reserves at this particular pit had been exhausted by the beginning of the 20th Century and it closed in 1908, but fascinatingly (well, to me,

5199 steams away from Kingsley & Froghall Churnet Valley Railway

Froghall Wharf: 1

Froghall Wharf: 2

at any rate) it had once been linked by a tramway and an inclined plain to a wharf on the Uttoxeter Canal. The last pit in Cheadle's coalfield, Foxfield, closed in 1965. The last pit in North Staffordshire, Silverdale closed in 1998. Our betters tell us that it's easier to get coal from Australia now as opposed to digging it up here.

Out in the countryside – how soon before we're told it's cheaper to *farm* in Australia than here? – they'd been spreading slurry on freshly silaged fields. It smelt like the Plasticine I used to play with as a child. Up above me the weather was improving. At Kingsley Holt (where the Staffordshire Way was crossed once again) a milestone intimidatingly spelt out the distances I still had to cover: Froghall 1, Ipstones 3, Onecote 7, Warslow 10, Longnor 14. Buxton 20, was over the border, and I could forget about it.

On reaching the centre of the village I was confronted by a sign which bore the challenging inscription: 'Road Ahead Closed'. I did what I always do in these circumstances, and pressed on. Experience has taught me that, more often than not, it will be possible to get through without much difficulty. Usually such signs are erected to give the road-menders a quiet life. On this occasion they were resurfacing. By gum, didn't those Clee Hill boys scatter like nine-pins as I roared through!

It was downhill all the way to Froghall, nestled

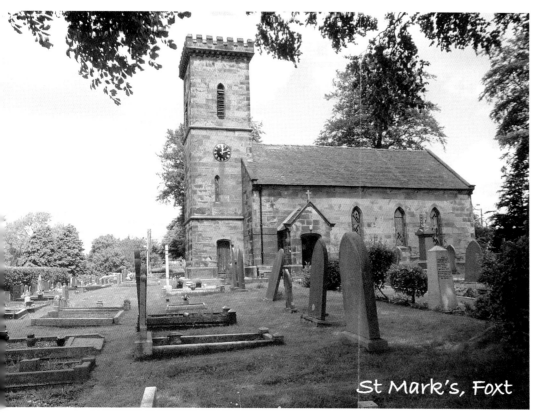
St Mark's, Foxt

village in which brick predominated. Half way up the twisting road I came upon a charming pub called the Woodcutters Arms. Charming, that was, until it dawned on me that it had long ago lost its licence and become merely an enviable dwelling. The name appeared with painted characters in relief above the entrance door. Apparently the pub served its last pint one melancholy day in 1975. For many years it had belonged to Joule's, the well known brewers in Stone.

deep in the endearing folds of the Churnet Valley. Frustratingly it was not one of the Churnet Valley Railway's operating days. It would have been enjoyable to obtain refreshment at the Station Café and watch one of the preserved line's steam locomotives going through the ritual of running round its train. Neither was there much life to be seen at Froghall Wharf, bucolic extremity of the Caldon Canal. All a far cry from its fire and brimstone days of smoking kilns and the noisy transhipment of lumps of limestone from tramway wagon to waiting narrowboat. The car park was empty, the usual rash of picnickers obviously disuaded by the ambivalence of the weather. They should have been more sanguine. It was now positively sunny and hot.

Hopefully it will not have escaped your notice that, thus far, forty-odd miles of increasingly undulating countryside have been traversed without recourse to dismounting and pushing. The same will not be true of the next seventeen miles. The by-road out of Froghall to Foxt ascends at what they now call 11%, but I can vouch for the fact that some of it is a good deal steeper. I had ventured a mere ten yards before being forced to get off and push. Froghall lies more or less on the 500 foot contour, Foxt is 750 feet above sea level, whilst the wastes of Black Heath beyond, are to be found a salutary 1,200 feet up. Suffice it to say, that I more or less walked all the way to the summit.

Foxt formed a palpable frontier. It was the last

Furthermore, I was too early for the Fox & Goose, so I pressed thirstily on, ignoring the supercilious comments of a llama in a neighbouring field, its Peruvian accent laced with a Staffordshire Moorlands dialect. I began to feel like a bed bug crawling over a crumpled counterpane. Not even an unfolding panorama over my shoulder, which featured The Wrekin on its horizon, could ameliorate the effort I was putting into the climb. Nearing the top at last, I overtook two slugs – just!

Now I found myself in a landscape of drystone walls and bog cotton. Could this be the same county? It seemed almost a season behind. There was still blossom on the hawthorn, and the cow parsley, long past its lacy best in the hedgerows I had left behind me, here remained lustrous and luxuriant. My spirits soared – like the lark in the neighbouring field – as I freewheeled down into Winkhill, pausing solely to peep over the stone parapet of the bridge which carries the road over the weed-strewn track of the old Leek and Waterhouses railway. 'It's a long time since stone trains rattled this way,' I thought to myself. 'No, it's much more environmentally-friendly for the output of Cauldon Quarry to go out by road,' replied my imaginary friend with ill-concealed irony. Entering Winkhill I crossed the River Hamps which, curiously, flows south before having a change of heart and turning north to make its way to its confluence with the Manifold.

'Alright?' called a friendly voice from a garden as I began to push the bike uphill out of Winkhill.

'I will be when I reach the top', came my laconic reply.

'I know how you feel,' the voice rejoined; obviously a fellow man of the road.

Halfway up the next hill a milk tanker growled by, and it was with some difficulty that I resisted a manic urge to grab its tailboard. At Waterfall Cross I entered the Peak National Park, though the landscape seemed impervious to this change in status. Nature's response was more subtle. There were late lambs in the fields, cattle with bells, and a continuing sense that this wasn't just another county, more another climate.

The buildings at Felthouse Farm were built of brick, and some gable ends, tile hung, which made it look as though it belonged to an entirely different location. I couldn't tell whether the signpost at the next road junction was beckoning me to a place called Ford, or simply warning me that there was a watersplash somewhere downhill out of sight. Grindonmoor Gate sounded as if it had escaped from the North York Moors and took me back to sun-parched and rain-soaked days in the Duke of Edinburgh's Award.

It seemed an unkind paradox that in pushing my bicycle slowly uphill the views were restricted, whereas going downhill, with the full panoply of a vista to admire, I would be going too quickly to do it justice. Thus it was that I hurtled into Butterton, barely taking in the tall steeple of its church, reminiscent of St Giles' in the context of its setting. Ignoring the instruction that cyclists should dismount and use the walkway, I plunged into the ford, which seemed to run down the road rather than across it. The road was cobbled under-

Barn on Grindon Moor

neath and slippery, and I belatedly saw the sense in the sign's advice, before falling off and getting my feet wet. A black dog raced out of a farm gate to admonish me. Fortunately its bark was worse than its bite. 'There's a good dog,' I said, soothingly.

'Get back oop that field,' roared its master, and before the dog could sheepishly obey, its mistress added her own, equally trenchant imprecation in a higher register.

Otherwise, Butterton was ghostly quiet. It brought to mind a village in the foothills of the Rhone Alps. Why, even the drains smelt French. In the past it would have been just as empty in the middle of the afternoon because most of the inhabitants would be out working in the fields. Now, I mused, they would be out working in call centres. But then a nice surprise, a post office store, in which I was able to purchase a sausage roll and a fizzy drink, welcome fuel seeing as how I hadn't had anything to eat or drink since Cheadle, four hours earlier.

Alpine overtones accompanied my exit from Butterton as well, now eastwards in the direction of Wetton Mill. Luxuriantly verged, the lane descended steeply past fields whose massed buttercups appeared to be waving like an excited crowd. Encouraged by such acclaim, I picked up speed and only resorted to my brakes when a sequence of potholes threatened to throw me over the handlebars. Not that it would have mattered, the banks of the Manifold when at last I reached the valley floor, were so thick in butterbur I would have had a cushioned landing. They serve teas and ices at the mill, and I refreshed myself with a lolly, dangling my legs over the water's edge and watching the antics of the mallards where the Manifold's clear waters are added to by Hoo

Butterton Ford

Brook.

The next two or three miles of my journey lay along the route of the former Leek & Manifold Valley Light Railway, a narrow gauge line closed as long ago as 1934, after just a brief thirty year lifespan, yet its ambience still permeates the valley and it is still fondly remembered in these parts. At first I had to share the way with cars, for after the rails had been taken up, the west bank of the Manifold was requisitioned for motor traffic. Even the old railway tunnel at Swainsley was adapted for road use. Fortunately, midweek before the main holiday season, interruptions to my progress were few and far between. Such has been the encroach of vegetation, since the railway builders cut a raw swathe through the valley, that it was difficult to tell where the cool natural 'tunnels' of green shade ended and the real tunnel commenced. But just before it swallowed me up, I glimpsed what I took to be a delightful circular folly down below me on the riverbank, and assumed it must have been an 'eye-catcher' for Swainsley Hall. At one time the hall (out of sight above the tunnel) belonged to Sir Thomas Wardle, the Leek dyer and advocate for the Pre-Raphaelite brotherhood and the Arts & Crafts movement. A mover and shaker of his time, amongst the guests he had entertained were 'Mark Twain' and Baden-Powell. I was interested to learn that he had a water-powered organ installed in the house. I was further interested to learn that he was a Director of the Leek & Manifold Valley Light Railway, but that had not stopped him insisting that a tunnel be provided to keep the railway out of the line of vision of Swainsley Hall.

Beyond the tunnel, the road reverts to the other side of the river and the old railway line is reserved for walkers and cyclists as it arcs round to Ecton. At one point I thought I heard the ghostly sound of an approaching train. Then I realised it was me, happily making the sort of chuff-chuff noises obviously not entirely forgotten from childhood.

It was at Ecton that the railway's promoters had high hopes of cashing-in on the copper traffic. But, as is often cruelly the case with such optimism, the copper mines ceased working before the railway could be opened. In the event, however, almost the only truly lucrative goods traffic did come from Ecton, and this was in the form of milk from the creamery that developed on the site of the old copper workings. Ingeniously, the difficulty of transhipping this traffic – where the narrow gauge tracks met their standard gauge counterparts at Waterhouses – was overcome by the provision of transporter wagons onto which standard gauge rolling stock could be shunted at Waterhouses for the journey along the light railway. In the line's brief heyday, milk left Ecton for London on a nightly basis. Bearing in mind a similar traffic on the Stafford

Old Station
Hulme End

Swainsley
Folly

to Uttoxeter line, perhaps it isn't sufficiently recognised how much of the county's dairy output was once destined for use in the capital.

Ah, but what a lovely sight the diminutive Leek & Manifold Valley trains must have made winding demurely through their precipitous valley. In the beginning the locomotives were dark red and the carriages primrose in colour. There was a sub-continental aspect about their design that lent them an outlandish appearance – the line's engineer, Everard Richard Calthrop, had cut his teeth on the Barsi Light Railway in India. What a shame the line didn't survive into the preservation era. Along with the lost likes of the Lynton & Barnstaple, the Southwold Railway and the Glyn Valley Tramway, it could have been one of the Great Little Railways of Britain now.

An embankment above a tussocky meadow brought me to the terminus at Hulme End. Heaping beauty above beauty, there had been aspirations that the line might have proceeded northwards to Buxton via Longnor. To no avail. Perhaps they ran out of money, perhaps they ran out of steam. The timber booking hall survives, in appropriate use as an information centre with toilet facilities, whilst a replica engine shed is used as a meeting room.

It was something of an anti-climax to return to the hurly-burly of the Queen's Highway. It was good to see Hulme End still supporting a village shop. A bridge carried me over the river by the Manifold Inn – once romantically known as the Light Railway Hotel, and apparently a bolt hole for the thirties film star, Robert Donat: Richard Hannay in Hitchcock's *The Thirty-nine Steps*.

I turned away from the Hartington road and headed uphill for Sheen. A farmer came down from the hillside on a quad-bike and turned into Lowside Farm. How these ubiquitous vehicles have revolutionised hill-farming. I could have done with one for the next half mile or so, for I was back plodding and pushing again, though the more slothful progress at least gave me the opportunity of paying closer attention to the wayside flowers, and gratifyingly even being able to name some of them: vetch, bird's-foot, knapweed and campion.

By Townend I was pedalling again. I passed a Wesleyan Chapel, a pub called the Staffordshire Knot, and a Youth Hostel by Peakstones Farm. Which brought me to Sheen, a village revered in tug-of-war circles. I could appreciate that. Up here they must have to make their own entertainment. A certain homogenity in architectural styling suggested that this was an estate village. Another uphill section ensued, but I found enough low gears to get me to the top. Cycling under the shoulder of Sheen Hill's rocky, triangulation pillar-topped peak I arrived at a straight length of road with a grandstand view over the neighbouring Dove. I remembered how I had once motored along the gated road to Pilsbury in a yellow Morgan savouring the 'delightful aroma of hot engine oil mingled with the musky smell of waving cow parsley'.

Lesser mortals might have dallied, but the straight road compelled momentum, and I sensed that the worst of the switchbacking was behind me. Now the road signs were obligingly counting down the miles to my destination. I saw a yellow field filled with black cattle and thought it would make appealing subject matter for a latter-day Van Gogh or Gauguin. I stopped to take a photograph of an

Edgetop, Longnor

enigmatic little roadside pillar at Knowsley Cross and was doubly rewarded with the unmistakable call of a curlew. The Staffordshire Moorlands provide a nesting habitat. Later in the year they would be heading for estuaries and coastal climes, but for the moment it was good to hear that haunting trill echoing across the countryside.

A mile further, and I was freewheeling into my final destination, the village of Longnor, just about as far as I could go in Staffordshire without breaking bounds. Village? Actually it used to be a market town, until the ebb and flow of the centuries left it high and dry on its windy ridge above the River Dove, buttressed and stone-built, peering robustly over the county boundary into Derbyshire. The old market hall functions as a craft shop and tea room now and there I repaired to slake my thirst with a

pot of tea. A trio of old boys had beaten me to it, *Last of the Summer Wine* look-alikes with their deadpan banter. A maternal waitress hovered solicitously over our manly needs, and cake was forthcoming. The crumbs left on our plates were, just that, crumbs of comfort.

It only remained for me to visit the last church of my journey, St Bartholomew's. I accessed it via narrow alleyways which might have doubled as Holmfirth, Haworth or Heptonstall. Aloof behind the Market Square, it dates from 1781, and, in its austerity, is the very antithesis of Hoar Cross, never mind Cheadle. And yet, once inside, and having passed the kitchen where a lady was washing vases, I felt it could not have been more symbolic of the harsh simplicity of life in these northern wastes. Back down there in the county's industrial heartland

St Bartholomew's, Longnor

they needed all the colour and ritual they could get. Up here a natural heaven was closer at hand. It needed only lustily, if unharmoniously, sung hymns frugally accompanied by violins, cello and bassoon to call down the angels. The churchyard is notable for being the location of the grave of William Billinge, a soldier who died in 1791 at the immense age of 112. He had enlisted in 1702 and saw action for the last time over forty years later, in helping to harry Bonnie Prince Charlie's Jacobites back out of the county in 1745.

Fifty-seven miles! Any serious lycra-clad cycling enthusiast could run that off in an afternoon. To take two days over it would be viewed as sissy in certain circles. But then, as I have hinted often enough in my canal and railway guide books, the essence of rewarding travel is frequent stopping and searching out. And a bicycle is a good mode of transport: environmentally; in terms of the fitness and well-being one derives from its use; and its adaptability: a halfway house between walking and driving. Already I was planning my next itinerary. Exactly how many miles of by-road, I wondered, are there in the county of Staffordshire?

Walking Backwards 1

'WHEN does the bus leave for Kinver?' I asked the driver of the number 228 drawn up in Bay E at Stourbridge bus station.

'One and half minutes ago,' he replied laconically. Not that he cared, he was otherwise engaged showing a colleague pictures of his Lake District holiday.

'We share a common interest,' explained the second bus man; 'fellwalking.'

'I'm off to do a bit of walking myself,' I said, not to be outdone. 'Not as high as Haystacks, mind you …the Staffordshire Way.'

'How long's that?' asked the second bus man.

'Ninety-two miles,' I replied off pat. 'But I'm only doing about twenty today; Kinver to Codsall.'

'*Twenty* miles from Kinver to Codsall,' he looked at me incredulously. 'It must wind about a bit.'

In the end we left about five minutes late, for one or two of the photographs depicted the driver's better half and she was a 'bit of all right!' It took twenty minutes to get to what used hyperbolically to be known as the 'Switzerland of the Midlands'. It was the Kinver Light Railway Company who coined the phrase for their own ends. It suited the operators of this quaint narrow gauge electric tramway to encourage day-trippers from the Black Country to pour into the picturesque south Staffordshire village and they duly came in their thousands. If only the KLR hadn't been abandoned in 1930, I might have reached Kinver rather more adventurously than by single decker bus, but that's the duplicity of Progress for you; nowadays Kinver's Light Operatic Society is better known than its Light Railway.

Kinver is still pretty and still popular and somehow doesn't feel like Staffordshire at all, never mind Switzerland. It is surprisingly large and contains a good deal of dormitory housing for people who work in the West Midlands conurbation but prefer – not entirely surprisingly – to pass their non-working hours in a more attractive setting. The High Street boasts far more shops and places of refreshment than would presumably be the case were it not for Kinver's continued attraction. Predicting that opportunities for refreshment might be scarce along the route of the Staffordshire Way, I dived into Isabelle's Bakery and obtained a sausage roll and a bottle of ginger beer. It wasn't in my nature to be pedantic where the Staffordshire Way was concerned. I fully intended to walk from one end of the county to the other: but, for a start, I was going to do it in the opposite direction to the guide book; and secondly, if anything caught my imagination 'off route' I would be open to temptation.

Technically, the walk begins or ends at the southern end of Kinver Edge where Staffordshire abuts Worcestershire. But to waste time walking in the opposite direction offended my sense of topography, so I started at the toposcope at the northern end of the Edge. Had it been a weekend afternoon I would have visited the Holy Austin rock houses which the National Trust have recently restored. The soft sandstone rock strata of the Stour valley has been conducive to hewing out accommodation for centuries. Indeed, there are still houses in the vicinity with back rooms that are effectively caves.

I took stock at the toposcope of all the directions I wouldn't be travelling in: the Clent and Lickey hills, Breedon Hill, the Malverns and Abberleys, the Clee hills, the Long Mynd and Wenlock Edge. For a wild moment I felt like a young man again, deliberating over my path through life, then realised it had already been chosen for me. It was bright in the west and grey in the east. Given a gentle westerly, I had high hopes of the day.

At ten o'clock I sidled unostentatiously down off the western flank of the Edge, descending through woodland humming with insects, several of who appeared quite prepared to drop everything and follow me all the way to Mow Cop. Back at road level, lesser mortals were emptying their car boots of picnic paraphernalia. I bid them a nonchalant hello, only just refraining from informing them that I was setting out to walk the whole of Staffordshire; it was too early for the signing of autographs.

Seeing forever – the view from Kinver Edge

Holy Austin Rock Houses

In planning to travel in the opposite direction to the official guide book, I had nervously wondered what the waymarking might be like in reverse. From the outset, such fears were allayed, the arrows with their Staffordshire Knot logo (yellow for footpaths, blue for bridleways) were well displayed in both directions. Thus it was that I soon felt confident enough to put the guide book back in my rucksack, relying entirely on my Ordnance Survey Explorer map and my eyes.

Skirting Kinver's self-effacing suburban periphery, the Staffordshire Way soon finds itself deep in the countryside, a line of electricity poles aiding navigation. From neighbouring hedgerows, I could have filled a carrier bag with ripe blackberries. A black cat passed propitiously across the path ahead of me. On one side lay a field of wheat; on the other, maize. White Hill Farm had been converted into a bijou residence, so bijou that it was up for sale. The way swung northwards, just within the perimeter of a belt of Scots pine. Nothing disturbed the silence save the occasional whirr of pigeon wings. The way became a sunken lane between outcrops of sandstone, sandy underfoot. It led across Compton Road, sleepily innocent of passing traffic.

The day was hotting up and I was beginning to warm to the task, falling into a rhythmic gait that must have been approaching three miles an hour. I mentally praised the original surveyors of the

Estate cottages, Enville

Staffordshire Way, they had chosen their route well – so far at least! On the edge of Lyndon Covert I came upon an enigmatic little cave, barred by a grill. I couldn't find any reference to it in the guide book. Presently the path became a track and I had to step aside to let a tractor pass. It made slightly less noise than the party of ramblers who followed in its wake. What is the collective noun for ramblers? It ought to be a 'gossip'.

From the map I divined that I was approaching Enville. At Home Farm the pond looked inviting. Gracious parkland of chestnut horses and chestnut trees ensued, followed by a side on view of the hall itself, grandiose home of the Earls of Stamford. The title is extinct but the house remains in the family, as it has done for over five hundred years. Furthermore it hasn't lowered its guard and let in the paying public; not, at least, on a regular basis. It is very much a working estate, extending to over six thousand acres, on land that rises to over six hundred feet where it nudges the Shropshire border. Amongst the sporting Earls was one who had his own race course, whilst another organised exhibition cricket matches against England XIs. There's still a cricket ground, and youngsters were enthusiastically practising their fielding as I passed.

A lengthy brick wall led me down to the village, where charming estate houses, though built of brick, appeared deceptively organic. I was an hour too

Scots pine, Enville

31

early for The Cat Inn, being especially disappointed not to be able to sample some Enville Brewery ale. Neither was there much to be had by way of sustenance at the Post Office, so I pressed on, passing out of the village on the A458, which briefly brought me back into the unwelcome world of speeding cars and vans. On the edge of the village stands the imposing church of St Mary, rubicundly built of local sandstone.

It was with some relief that I left the road, but it was relief short-lived. Surreally passing through the private grounds of Enville Court, the Way promptly plunged into a boggy wood, squelchy underfoot. Thriving in the gloom and damp, nettles stretched their treacherous stems and stinging leaves across the path and made me regret the wearing of shorts. The gods, I guessed, had come to the conclusion that I'd had things too easy. They were playing with me. For no sooner had I emerged from the wood than I found myself faced with a farm gate that cattle were obviously in the habit of congregating by. Quagmire was an understatement. My trainers were swallowed up, mud and slurry coagulated around my ankles. At first I tried to pick my way judiciously around this morass. In the end I gave up and trudged through it. Up in their Olympian heights the gods wet themselves laughing.

Presently I emerged from this Bunyanesque Slough of Despond and found myself on firmer ground, both literally and metaphorically. A covey of female pheasants came out of the undergrowth and accompanied me for a few yards; twittering handmaidens, like something out of a novel by Barbara Pym. A brief woodland interlude ensued, climaxed by a timber bridge spanning Philley Brook. In the next field I had company, a herd of cattle marshalled by a hefty bull with a nursery tale ring through his nose. Two alpha males in one field, something had to give. But for the cowpats, I'd have shown him a clean pair of heels.

I'd got my breath and dignity sufficiently back to bid the young girl who came out of the gate of Lutley Farm on a horse 'good morning'. But she was not destined to fall in with me on my Pilgrim's Progress for she continued clip-clopping along the metalled road, whilst I turned into a potato field.

If you want the honest truth, bulls don't really frighten me at all, but llamas do. Thus it was with some trepidation that I made my way past Mere Hall where I encountered a sizeable contingent of the species. The root of my discomfort lies in an incident on holiday in northern France when one appeared suddenly over a hedge and spat at me. A notice at the edge of the field

Rushton Spencer
The Cloud
Congleton Edge
Rudyard Lake
Staffordshire Moorlands
Mow Cop
×Leek
Kidsgrove
Caldon Canal
Cheddleton
Churnet Valley
Consall Forge
Kingsley
Weaver Hills
Kingsley Holt
Cheadle
Alton
Denstone
Rocester
Dove Valley
Uttoxeter
Needwood Forest
Blithfield Reservoir
Trent & Mersey Canal
Great Haywood
Abbots Bromley
Stafford×
Shugborough
Colton
Shropshire Union Canal
Staffs & Worcs Canal
Glacial Boulder
Rugeley
Penkridge
Cannock Chase
Mitton
Bickford Meadows
Lapley
Cannock
aqueduct
Brewood
Chillington Hall
Codsall
Wolver-hampton
Seisdon
Staffs & Worcs Canal
Vineyard
Halfpenny Green
Highgate Common
×Dudley
Enville Hall
Enville
Kinver Edge
×Stourbridge
Kinver
North

32

beside the Staffordshire Way jocularly reassured passers-by that one of Mere Hall's llamas, by the name of 'Guinness', didn't spit, but that, as far as I was concerned, implied that the rest did, and it was with some relief that I put two irrigation pools between me and those expectorating Peruvian interlopers.

Stability returned with the stucco frontage of Leaton Hall, and beyond it, what I took to be The Wrekin. Then my focus fell upon the undulating runways and assorted hangars of Halfpenny Green aerodrome, laid out during the Second World War, and still made use of by light aircraft, helicopters and sky-divers. Expansion of the site commensurate with commercial flying has been on the cards for a number of years, though not without hostility from the natives. All a far cry from its early years as a base for the ponderous Blackburn Botha reconnaissance plane and torpedo bomber. Prince William of Gloucester died in an air race at Halfpenny Green in 1972.

I was growing hungry and thirsty and it was slowly dawning on me that if I stayed true to the Staffordshire Way the opportunity of responding to either need would not arise until I reached Seisdon, five miles and the best part of two hours further on, and even that relied on the pub being open. Scanning the map, I was intrigued by the existence of a vineyard at Halfpenny Green, so I decided to head there. The waymarked route would take me reasonably close to the vineyard, and I would have been happy sticking with it had it not been overgrown with bracken fronds on reaching the entrance to Highgate Common. That made my mind up for me, I took to the road, skirting the perimeter of the aerodrome through Gospel Ash.

The Royal Oak was open at Halfpenny Green itself, but by that point, I had pictured raising a glass of chilled local wine

Halfpenny Green Vineyard

to my lips and was not about to be sidetracked. Half a mile's brisk walking brought me to the eponymous vineyard, reassuringly advertising refreshments. Goodness it looked busy too. As I made my way up the drive a number of cars drove in and out. The restaurant and tea rooms appeared equally busy, mostly with what looked like retired couples tucking into generously portioned plated meals.

'I was wondering if I could just have a snack in the garden,' I confided to the woman behind the counter.

'We only serve cakes and teas in the garden, sir,' came her well-rehearsed reply.

I assumed my little-boy-lost look and her maternal instincts kicked in.

'Tell you what,' she suggested, in a delightful, western edge of Black Country burr, 'we'll call it a takeaway. Choose something from the sandwich menu and we'll quietly slip it out to you.'

'And do you serve your own wine by the glass?' I asked, rewarding her enterprise with my seasoned man-of-the-world look.

'What size would that be, sir?'

'Oh, large I think: very large.'

The wine was so large it cost more than the smoked salmon sandwich, but it was chilled and delicious and dry in equal measure. I sat in the garden against a backdrop of vines half suspecting I must have been suffocated by bracken on Highgate Common and arrived in heaven's waiting room. Surreptitiously I pinched myself, but didn't feel a thing, though I did notice my glass was already half empty. They've been tending vines at Halfpenny Green since 1983 and the estate now runs to twenty-five acres. They also offer guided tours and self-guided tours, as well as craft workshops and coarse fishing. Indeed I suspect for many regulars the business does represent an earthly heaven.

An outfit on the

vineyard site offers electric bike hire, and I dare say I was tempted as I tore myself away. Rejoining the route of the Staffordshire Way, I crossed the B4176 in baking heat, before plunging into a refreshingly cool belt of woodland which clings to a ridge known as Abbot's Castle Hill.

Geologists will tell you, in tones approaching exultant, that this escarpment consists of the same Bunter Pebble Beds which form Kinver Edge, and that they originate from the Triassic period of the Mesozoic era. Me? I'm just content to bask in the beauty on view, in the same way that I'm content to appreciate the handsome qualities of a locomotive without necessarily knowing all its engineering terms, or to admire a delicate bosom without being aware what fatty tissues make it up.

The landscape falls precipitously away into Shropshire to the west of Abbot's Castle Hill, and between the ivied boles of birch trees I saw Titterstone Clee and Brown Clee in all their glory. To the east, not quite so appealingly, stood the high-rise citadels of Dudley and Wolverhampton. 'Go West young man, go west' urged a voice within, but I was too old and set in my ways to heed it.

Tinker's Castle Farm had lots of piebald horses and a delightful Dutch barn clad in corrugated iron. A couple were picking blackberries from the hedgerow at the far end of the hill, and it looked like they'd amassed a bumper crop. I struck left along a lane marked private to Wolmore Farm; private, that is, where motorists are concerned. It would have been easier to go straight down the road into Seisdon, for the next section of the footpath lay along a narrow, fenced-off strip at the edge of a field. This approach may have suited the farmer, but it left the path somewhat overgrown. I began to long for moleskin breeches. One particularly aggressive bramble wrestled me into a neck hold. The shade of an oak provided a brief interregnum where ground vegetation had insufficient light to flourish. But soon I was battling my way along the edge of that blessed field again, mouthing imprecations at farmers and the people whose job it is to maintain rights of way, if such people exist.

On the outskirts of Seisdon a huge poultry farm stood eerily abandoned by the path, as though the chickens had one day organised a mass break out and had never been recaptured. Round a corner I came upon a little brick built electricity relay station, nicely emblazoned with the bas-relief badge of its original owner 'MEC', the Midland Electricity Co. Strolling into the village I saw a man bare-chested and bronzed weeding his garden, and figured he more likely derived that tanned torso from a climate more reliably filled with sunshine than Seisdon's.

Smestow Brook was an old friend I had encountered on many occasions exploring the Staffordshire & Worcestershire Canal which it parallels further downstream. I paused to look over the low parapet of the bridge which spanned its clear sandy bed and was tangentially put in mind of Richard Hannay's meeting with Sir Walter Bullivant on the banks of the Kennet in John Buchan's *The Thirty-nine Steps*. I half expected Sir Walter to emerge from the pretty whitewashed cottage nearby whistling a bar or two of *Annie Laurie* but he didn't materialise. By the entrance to Seisdon House, however, I was rewarded with a Victorian post box.

At a big house called The Elms I left the road, glad that I wasn't responsible for keeping its huge sward of lawn mown. A disintegrating security fence hinted at abandoned sand pits and then I came to a succession of paddocks in which horses were coralled by dint of electric fences which always make me nervous. A stile brought me into a field of desiccated oil seed rape, in which a pathetic attempt had been made to clear a path. In the next field I was almost knee high in yellow vetch. Beyond Furnace Grange Farm, with its big brick farmhouse and array of accompanying outbuildings, I came upon Smestow Brook again, gurgling by pungent clusters of balsam. Two marching lines of electricty pylons led me to Trescott.

I reckoned I had covered about thirteen miles and was glad to be travelling south to north with the sun on my neck and not in my eyes. Noting a colourful cottage garden, I darted between speeding cars on the Wolverhampton to Bridgnorth road and joined a farm track grandiloquently known as 'Shop Lane', the only other occupant of which was a free-range chicken. I pressed on, noting from the map that the Staffordshire Way would soon be interweaved with the Monarch's Way, a circuitous waymarked path inspired by King Charles II's escape route from Worcester to Shoreham-on-Sea in 1651. At 615 miles in length, it put the 92-mile Staffordshire Way in its place.

After a mile or so in the open, I was glad to reach Toadsnest Lane, a sunken bridleway offering plenty of shade. According to the guide book the lane contains a variety of common ground plants, such as dog's mercury, yellow archangel, red campion, ground ivy, cleavers and white deadnettle. Would that I were able to distinguish between them, but at school they prioritised on square roots and the exports of Venezuela at the expense of wild flowers and the stars.

Crossing Pattingham Road made me think of the annual Bells of Pattingham cross country race that I enjoy taking part in. It takes place in October and always seems to usher in autumn. Arm in arm, the two long distance paths sauntered around the margins of a golf course. In the guide book there was reference to some ruined buildings which had been a Dutch Army base during the Second World War. They appeared to be in the process of being refurbished as modern dwellings, but there was a sad absence of activity, as if the project had been hit by the recession, and the money had run out.

A line of poplars led to Wrottesley Hall and another golf course. I must have momentarily lost concentration, for I began to harbour suspicions that I had taken the wrong turn and had to retrace my steps for a quarter of a mile. My instincts were right, I had missed a stile well hidden by an avenue of trees. I don't like losing my way at the best of times, and was glad that no one had witnessed my *faux pas*.

Obviously the smartly accoutred denizens of the golf club like to keep the less presentable rambling fraternity out of sight and mind, for the path is routed through dense undergrowth to the rear of the club house. It zigzagged between fallen boughs, stagnant pools and clumps of nettles, and I was stung several times. Even on the other side, matters scarcely improved, for the path was hemmed in between a wheat field and the wall that divided it from the A41. So exasperated with the second class facilities meted out to walkers was I, that I failed to savour the historical significance of Thomas Telford's Holyhead road.

It was a relief to cross the main road and to find myself on a metalled lane leading down into the little village of Oaken. Here the Staffordshire Way and the Monarch's Way went their different ways, and I gratefully trudged down a quiet backwater called Oaken Drive to the end of the first leg of my journey at Codsall railway station. I had covered the best part of twenty miles and would have relished a glass of Holdens in the pub which now occupies the charmingly Italianate station building. But, as luck would have it, there was only five minutes to wait for the train, hardly enough for even a practised quaffer of ale such as me to down a pint.

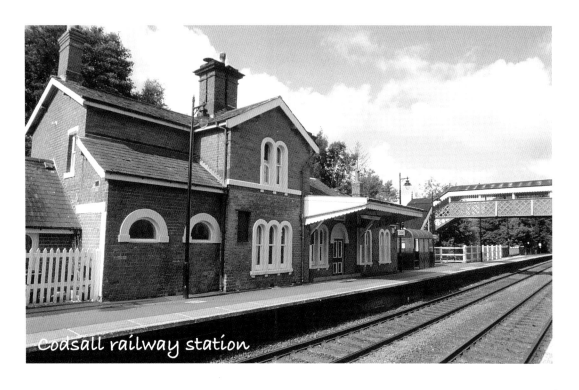

Codsall railway station

Bottle kilns, Gladstone Museum

Six Towns
One Ticket

I must have been fourteen when my Mother casually let drop the existence of the Five Towns novels of Arnold Bennett. They were not her usual fare. She preferred biographies. Serendipitously I found a clutch of them on the shelves of the school library. Uniform Methuen editions in red and white dust jackets: largely unread, if their pristine pages were anything to go by; the school's most popular reading matter being invariably characterised by a patina of ink stains, greasy fingerprints, and biscuit crumbs.

Though it lay just twenty-five miles to the north-west of where I was growing-up, the district of which Bennett had written was known to us not as the Five or Six Towns, but as The Potteries, a smoky, shadowy, industrialised enclave which we had only penetrated on one unforgettable occasion, to see an early showing of *The Sound of Music* at the Hanley Odeon. We drove back haunted by images of edelweiss and alpine meadows, not bottle kilns and colliery headstocks. As initial reconnaissance trips go, it was a wasted opportunity.

Thus it was that I had to rely on the not inconsiderable power of Bennett's prose to evoke my first vivid impressions of North Staffordshire's industrial heartland, and to this day I find myself absentmindedly and subconsciously referring to Turnhill, Bursley, Hanbridge, Knype and Longshaw, as opposed to Tunstall, Burslem, Hanley, Stoke and Longton. Fenton, it was apocryphally maintained, had been ignored because the author's mother-in-law hailed from there. Later I learned, more authoritatively, that Bennett simply thought that Five, with its open vowel, sounded better than Six.

Arnold Bennett's Five Towns were as real to me as Thomas Hardy's Wessex and D. H. Lawrence's Nottinghamshire. More enjoyable in that I didn't have to study them at O or A Level for, inexplicably (but thankfully) the examining boards obviously considered Bennett too minor a talent to be worthy of study. Perhaps they were fooled by Bennett's tongue in cheek observation that the district was characterised by 'excessive provincialism'. From where the adolescent version of me was standing, it was impossible to get enough of the intoxicating cocktail of parochiality and provincialism.

For reasons unapparent to me still, I didn't go back to The Potteries after that initial foray to the cinema until I was a student at art school, intent on taking photographs of pot banks before they vanished. As a subject for my paintings, I had become enamoured of bottle kilns, or ovens as I liked to term them. Some of my canvases consisted of little else. Freud would have had a field day.

Entering the district from the east along the old A50, I did not have far to go before encountering a cluster of bottle kilns on the hill which slopes down into Longton. Moreover there was plenty of time to regard them, in those days the traffic through Longton moved at a snail's pace. Forty years later the road past the Gladstone Works was uneerily quiet as I made my approach. Furthermore it was no longer a Works, it was a Museum! 'Perhaps I belong in a museum as well,' I thought, as I purchased my entry ticket. The last time I was here the pot bank resembled the *Marie Celeste*, and I had been able to take my photographs for free.

Gladstone Pottery Museum is one of Stoke-on-Trent's most successful visitor attractions. 'No visit to the city would be complete without experiencing this unique museum' claims the tourist blurb, and this had obviously been taken literally by a coach party of Germans whose earnest body I tagged along with, first sitting through a brief introductory film whose finer points I was able to elucidate for my closest neighbours. Certain salient facts lodged themselves in my brain. In no particular order these were that: the manufacture of pottery goods flourished in the district due to the local availability of clay and coal and water; that Longton specialised in fine bone china; and that at the turn of the 19th and 20th centuries the life expectancy in Longton was a paltry forty-six, a statistic that was not much improved upon before the passing of the Clean Air Act fifty years later.

The film drew to its conclusion and we trailed blinking out into the sunlit yard, gathering in brittle knots between the curvaceous thighs of the buxom kilns. There was a certain Teutonic briskness about their tour guide which I could not help but admire. Questions were not encouraged. Perhaps they had a hectic schedule. Whatever the reason, we did not linger over-long in any one section of the museum, let alone pour over any one exhibit. From the Engine Room to the Slip House, through the Mould Maker to the Colour Gallery we were marched, our receptive senses a blurr of jiggers and jolleyers, dippers and gilders, mill men and pug men, places, drawers and bedders. Goodness knows what the German translation for saggar makers bottom knockers is, but knowing that nation's predilection for joining words together it's likely to be impressive!

I sensed that the ladies of the party might have liked to chance their much bejewelled arms at throwing a pot, or making a china flower, but were put off by the tour guide's tendency to click his heels and utter a prompt 'schnell' at any who dared hover. The sections devoted to tiles and toilets were equally quickly disposed of. The latter's realistic aromas not the source of vulgar humour they would have been to an English coach party. We ended our tour in the Doctor's House. I felt queasy enough merely loitering in the waiting room. In the surgery itself, the doctor was advising a woman in the early throes of pregnancy that termination was out of the question, even if it was her tenth!

Queen's Park

The brochure had advised a minimum of two and a half hours to do the museum justice. The Germans and I did it in forty-five minutes. They were making for the Lake District, I had the whole of The Potteries to explore.

There could hardly be greater contrast between the 19th Century environs of Gladstone Works and the futuristic overtones of Longton's bus station, though I felt I knew which most balanced observers would prefer. On the way down I'd encountered the indoor market in full swing. They fascinate me, these throwbacks to a more innocent retailing age, and I was tempted to dally, but the morning was marching on, and I had five more towns to visit.

First Group have a stranglehold on public transport in the Potteries these days. Well perhaps not a stranglehold, let alone a monopoly, but a painful arm-lock for sure. Not that I am dog-matically against monopolies. Nost-algically you knew where you were when every mun-icipality operated its own bus comp-any. By livery alone you could make a decent stab at guessing the locality, had you been led blindfolded into any given market place before hav-ing your sight restored. In the iconoclastic Potteries it was inevitable that they would have their own cherished bus operator, just as an earlier gen-eration had re-joiced in The Knotty, the district's indigen-ous railway company.

Despite the mildly embarrassing connotations of its initials, the Potteries Motor Traction Company symbolised the region it so loyally represented to the extent that, when it lost its independence in the wake of Margaret Thatcher's meddlesome deregulation of bus services, something more than just its red and cream (or latterly red and yellow) paintwork vanished. Waiting under the cavernous, yet altogether anonymous and impersonal, steel and glass canopy for my bus to Fenton, as a succession of colourless First Group vehicles came and went, I wished I had been making the journey forty or fifty years earlier, not just for the industrialised landscapes I would not now happen upon, but the vanished conveyances that would not carry me there either.

When the bus came blandly in and braked to a halt with a sigh, it seemed to genuflect in the process. I stepped aboard and asked for a day ticket which would enable me to get on and off as I pleased. It seemed astonishing value at just four pounds and twenty pence. Though why the twenty pence? Was it merely there to give the driver a reason to look aggrieved, or to grumble if you failed to tender the exact fare? A fiver would speed up the transaction, yet still represent a good deal.

The bus rose from its haunches, reversed out from beneath the canopy, took a big deep breath, then departed with a growl, joining the road and making its way through the inevitable periphery of retail stores and fast food outlets: Five Towns, Six Towns? – it could have been anywhere. My fellow passengers appeared oblivious, they had probably made the journey a million times and ceased to care or notice. They were thinking about what they were going to have for lunch, and who to put their money on in the three-thirty at Uttoxeter.

Peering assiduously out of the window I spotted a fish & chip shop called Dresden Fisheries. Later I discovered that the suburb of Dresden had been developed in the middle of the 19th Century from land owned by the Duke of Sutherland. Local historians can find no evidence of the name's derivation, but can only assume that it comes from the German city's tradition of porcelain manufacture.

Presently we came to the ornate entrance gates of a park. Queen's Park, I gleaned from the large scale map in my possession. I glimpsed a clocktower and tennis courts as the bus turned into an avenue of limes fronting substantial Victorian villas. What lost graciousness lay in their facades. Some moulded window arches were inlaid with the sort of decorative tiles on display at the Gladstone Pottery Museum. It pleased me to think that such items were still at large and not yet wholly preserved in aspic.

At the foot of that bosky avenue we passed what I took to be a war memorial and turned left on to the main road to Trentham. We passed

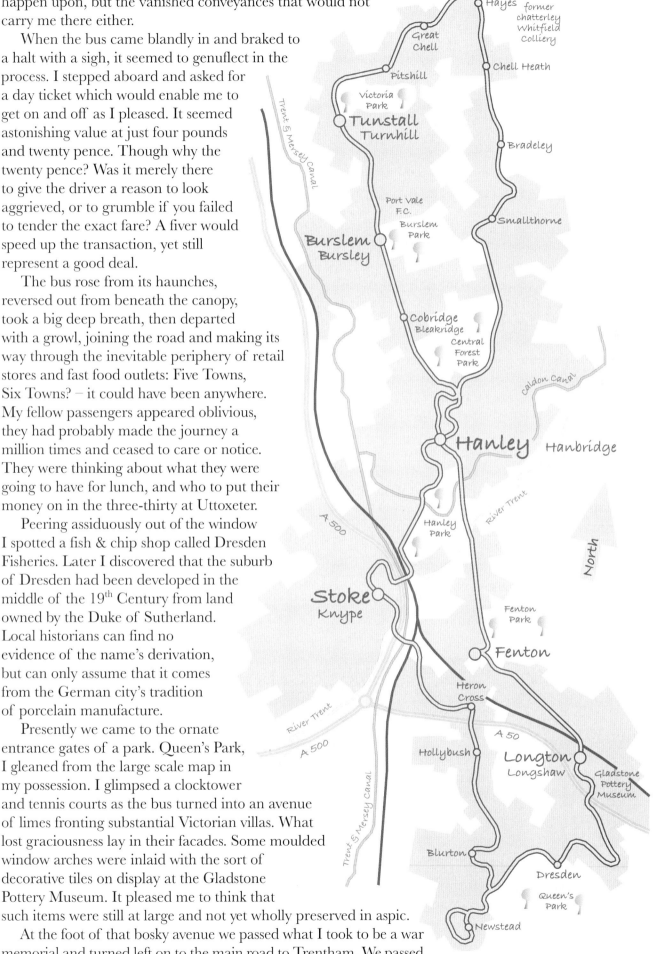

beneath an old railway bridge which reference to my old one inch Ordnance Survey map showed as once having connected Florence Colliery to the main line. Diligent research later revealed that Florence Colliery was one of the last mines to stay open in the area, lasting until 1990, though in latter years it had been merged with the mine at Hem Heath and was used largely for access and ventilation. Oh, and by the way, it derived its pretty name from one of the Duke of Sutherland's daughters. The map showed it skirting the bottom edge of Queen's Park by the boating lake. I would have liked a time machine to transport me back where, blazered and boatered, with a parasol-shaded companion, I might have shipped the oars to watch a softly puffing train of coal wagons clatter along the embankment.

Florence Colliery coal wagon, Foxfield

Back in the utilitarian present, the bus turned off the main road into a housing estate called Newstead. My old map showed only a farm. The first sign of humanity I spotted was a female police officer on patrol. The bus weaved its way deeper and deeper into the labyrinthine conglomeration of avenues, greens, groves, drives, walks and roads. I expected to meet a Minotaur at any moment. It came in the unlikely shape of a long-haired youth with a guitar slung over his back who, dispensing with small talk, simply demanded of the driver: 'You goana ta Stoke mate?'

For my part I was beginning to forget where I was going. On the map Fenton looked little more than a mile from Longton. Diverting as the journey had been to date, and even allowing for the waywardness of bus routes, we seemed to be taking a disproportionate amount of time to get there.

The next stop on the mystery trip was another estate. This one was called Blurton. The bus bounced over a succession of speed humps so violently that the youth dropped his guitar. I wondered idly what all the occupants of these houses did for a living. Or didn't they anymore? We went back under the old railway line. The authorities obviously hadn't bothered to take the old bridges away, unless they had a masterplan up their sleeves for a cycleway.

Hollybush, and more houses. Gradually we were creeping up on Fenton from behind. I was reassured. The housing grew in size. There were drives – many of them with more than one car parked affluently – and well-tended front gardens, each trying to outdo its neighbour in the elaboration of its floral display. We crossed the A50, a dual-carriagewayed artery beetling with through traffic.

And then I got a nasty shock. For instead of carrying straight on, we turned left, the compass set for Stoke! Doubt increasing, I rummaged in my rucksack for the route diagram I'd nonchalantly put away, convinced that it was a No.23A that I needed. Removing my glasses, and trying to ignore the potholes which the bus seemed determined to wallow in, self-pityingly, I saw that I had mistakenly boarded a 23A instead of a 28A!

Heron Cross Bottle Kiln

Less seasoned travellers might have panicked. Displaying remarkable self-control, I adjusted myself internally to the notion that I was now going to Stoke. After all, hadn't chance toyed playfully with some of the world's greatest explorers. Sitting phlegmatically still as the 23A careered down into Stoke, I knew I could hold my own in such exalted company as Odysseus, Vasco de Gama, Scott of Antarctica or Michael Palin.

Stoke gave every appearance of being a foreign country in any case. Another planet even. The bus dropped me by the old market hall, destroyed by fire on Cup Final Day 1982 according to an interpretive plaque by the entrance. Now it appeared to have reinvented itself as a library, an impression confirmed by two helpful librarians, Moira and Jill, who, perhaps having been on a council-sponsored course to recognise lost souls when they saw one, proceeded to take me in hand.

They seemed amused by the notion that I was travelling through the district by bus.

'You're juiced here for the day, then?' they cooed.

'But it's beginning to feel like a lifetime,' I quipped, buying peals of laughter.

'We're only juiced getting used to being here ourselves,' confessed Moira, when I asked if they had a copy of the Heritage Trail leaflet. 'There isn't rheum here to put the full range out anymore. There was more rheum in the old library.'

I refrained from making the obvious remark, and

encouraged her to continue.

'It's worth going to look at the old library,' she trilled, pronouncing 'look' as in the biblical correspondent Luke. 'It had a balcony, but we had trouble with boys spitting from it. And when they weren't up on the balcony spitting off it, they were down under it luke-ing up ladies' dresses.'

'That sounds like my sort of library,' I said, with the sort of smirk I thought was expected of me.

Meanwhile, Jill had been busy printing off some material for me, and thrust a wodge of papers enthusiastically my way with a: 'That should keep you going!'

For her part, Moira seemed tickled with the idea that I planned to visit each of the Six Towns in turn.

'Our old Head Librarian was once asked to send a parcel of books up to Burslem,' she said, delightfully pronouncing books as if it rhymed with Luke's again. 'Someone said he ought to take them up himself on the boose. He turned and gave them a horrified Luke, saying: 'Boot, I've never been that far before.'

I felt duty bound to go and see the old library out of loyalty to Moira and Jill. Alas it was boarded-up, awaiting a vote on its future. Perhaps they'd turn it into an indoor market.

The most peculiar thing about Stoke – and it's important here to emphasise that there exists what amounts to an hierarchy of peculiarities – is that it doesn't resemble a town at all. Strangers stepping from the sleek Manchester or London bound Virgin

Stoke's 'old' Library

Pendolinos, which arrive and depart from the railway station at half-hourly intervals throughout the day, are entitled to feel nonplussed at the absence of any of the usual trappings of commercial activity. Sainsbury's apart, the shops are self-effacing, scattered, and independently owned. The locals are hugely delighted by this sleight of hand. They never wanted to be part of a confederation in any case. Alright, the youngsters might flock to the chain stores up in Hanley, always assuming they can afford to go. But, the older they get, the inhabitants revert to their distinct townships and stay there, cocking a snook at their five neighbours, they never trusted them in the first place! I wandered back to the bus stop and waited for a bus to take me to the aforementioned metropolis, Hanley. And what do you know, it was a 23A again. I was beginning to feel like a character in *Groundhog Day*.

Hanley Park

I found myself perched in front of an elderly couple with Welsh accents who kept up a running commentary like excited children.

'We're off!' squealed the woman as the bus was set in motion.

'Another adventure!' rejoiced her husband.

'Ooh look, there's Spode,' cried the wife.

'Closed down now,' lamented the man.

It would be tedious to reproduce their whole output. Goodness knows the novelty soon wore off for at least one eavesdropper. We went over the A500, stopped outside the railway station – 'there's the station love!' – then turned right past the premises of Staffordshire University, a not unimposing pile with a frieze above its front door. Then we were traversing a pocket of Asian food shops and fashion outlets, a little subcontinent, sufficient to itself between the station and Hanley's leafy park. We came to a halt by a parcel of allotments.

'Ooh look at those potatoes,' said the Welsh woman.

'A sight for sore eyes,' rejoined her spouse.

They jumped with joy when we turned right at the next junction, delighted by the bus's waywardness.

'We'll have to bring a compass next time,' cried the man.

'And I'll have to bring a revolver next time,' I thought privately.

Who could resist the urge to alight in Hanley's self-proclaimed Cultural Quarter? Not I! As the bus whisked the old couple off to even giddier heights, I crossed the road and entered the august portals of the City Museum & Art Gallery. When it opened – the best part of thirty years ago now – the City of Stoke-on-Trent had every right to be proud of their new acquisition. And although time may have robbed it of some of its chutzpah and panache, I never find it a less than fascinating way to spend the odd half hour or so when I'm in town. The galleries devoted to flora and fauna, geology and ancient history, are undoubtedly excellent in their way, but my tastes are more culturally-focussed, and I invariably make a bee-line for the Spitfire Gallery in which resides RW388, a representative of Reginald Mitchell's peerless fighter plane.

Mitchell was born in the district (if indeed Kidsgrove *counts* as the district!) in 1895, hence the aeroplane's presence in the museum. It is one of over twenty thousand built between 1938 and 1947, of which two hundred or so survive, fifty of which are still able to fly. RW388 was built at Castle Bromwich in 1945 and was never used in combat. It last flew in 1952. I trust this data isn't boring you, there is history behind the numbers. Permit me to give you one more number: during the Battle of Britain the average life expectancy of a Spitfire pilot in the air was a mere eighty-severn hours!

Four of The Potteries most famous sons have wall-space devoted to them. In ascending order of obscurity they are: the photographer, William Blake; the composer, Havergal Brian; the author, Arnold Bennett; and the footballer, Sir Stanley Matthews.

William Blake (1874-1957) ran a stationery shop in Longton and dabbled in photography as a lucrative sideline. Scenes of exquisite ugliness and beauty were readily available on his doorstep. Arguably my favourite depicts Edensor Marl Hole, a gargantuan declivity, not unlike a crater on the moon, into which the terraced streets and phalanxed pot banks of Longton appear about to fall as soon as the exposure is done. Bruegel couldn't have dreamed it up. But Blake's oeuvre wasn't entirely industrial. He was equally skilled in capturing pastoral scenes, whether municipal as in the public parks of the Six Towns, or rural, as far distant as the Staffordshire Moorlands. I envy him in two respects: his talent, and his era.

Havergal Brian (1876-1972) is not widely known even amidst the arcane and silty backwaters of classical music: you won't find his works on the shelves of HMV shops between Beethoven and Brahms, let alone Bax and Britten. He belongs, rather, in the same eccentric mould as America's Charles Ives. He was born in the Dresden I had just passed through, to working-class parents, and was almost entirely self-taught. He was fortunate, however, to find a wealthy patron – one of the Mintons – which did much to mitigate against the indifference and misunderstanding his compositions encountered. His output included an astonishing thirty-two symphonies, most notably *The Gothic*, a work requiring two hundred instrumentalists, four soloists, a choir of five hundred, and a bird scarer. Scant wonder he was seldom performed anywhere, never mind in the Six Towns.

Arnold Bennett (1867-1931) deserves more than the 'corner' devoted to him. He was born at 90 Hope Street, Hanley but later moved with his parents to more salubrious surroundings at 205 Waterloo Road, Cobridge, halfway between Hanley and Burslem. Amidst the meagre exhibits of his lifetime are a Gladstone bag and a pair of slippers. Several of his delicate watercolours hang from the wall. He was a better writer than a painter. When I last looked him casually up on Amazon his most popular book, *The Old Wives' Tale*, was in 37,222[th] position in their sales chart, 18,219 places behind my *Canal Companion to the Oxford & Grand Union Canals*, a statistic which said more about the inadequacies of the book-buying public than our respective merits as writers. In my humble opinion *The Card* is even more amusing than *Three Men in a Boat*. How gratifying that both men

hailed from the overlooked county of Staffordshire.

Sir Stanley Matthews (1915-2000) needs no introduction from me. Suffice it to say that he retired from professional football at the astonishing age of fifty, never having been booked!

Sated with history and culture, I left the museum and sought to gratify a baser human instinct, hunger. Fortunately I was not unacquainted with The Atrium, a café incorporated within Victoria Hall. There, I knew, I could treat myself to a brace of cheese and bacon oatcakes for the throwaway price of two pounds and twenty-five pence. I consumed them at a pavement table, chuckling to myself at the thought of what Arnold Bennett – a sophisticate of Paris – might have made of his disciple's éclat.

Hanley's bus station lies cheek by jowl with the Cultural Quarter, though a good deal seems lost, culturally, in translation. The buses depart in a mocking echo of the Le Mans 24 Hour Race; reversing out, grinding their gears, and disappearing in a cloud of noxious fumes. I walked up and down, perusing the departure boards, knowing full well that I wanted to get to Tunstall, but wanting to do it as romantically and adventurously as possible. Two destinations in particular fired my imagination – Talke Pits and Fegg Hayes – there is poetry to be found in the humblest, most unpromising of circumstances.

I peered more intently at the network diagram this time, and divined that I needed a No.29. I was its sole occupant save for two boys on the back seat who must have been all of twelve summers old at the most.

'I used to love riding on buses when I was little,' confided one to the the other.

I hoped he was enjoying himself as much as I was. We threaded our way through Hanley's commercial heart, gaining more passengers at a stop outside the Potteries Shopping Centre. It didn't seem to take us long to shake off Hanley, however, and soon we were skirting the green periphery of Central Forest Park, a popular leisure facility on regenerated land once devoted to coal mining. A vast cemetery preceded Smallthorne, a tangled thoroughfare of pharmacies and convenience stores made memorable for me by the sight of Darlow's Bait & Tackle emporium. At the next stop two young women struggled aboard with pushchairs in which their respective offspring were busily engaged in sucking ice lollies.

'If you don't finish that lolly I'll chuck it out of the window,' admonished one.

Not to be outdone, her companion shrieked: 'Give it here and stop rubbing it in your eyes.' Ah the joys of motherhood. Averting my horrified gaze, I caught sight of a pub called The Swan, balefully boarded-

Former Post Office

The Wizard of the Dribble

Former Meat Market

up and bearing the legend: 'closed due to lack of interest'.

We turned left at Ford Green and headed through Bradeley to Chell Heath where a pub called the Knave of Clubs had a scrap of paper pinned to the door which read 'toilets for customers only' ... I wondered how many toilets patronised it on an average day.

On the surface of it, Fegg Hayes was an anticlimax. On first acquaintance it appeared to consist of ex-mineworker's cottages, washing lines and feral gangs of unemployed youths. The Miner's Welfare – rechristened Sports & Social Club – dated from AD 1929. To its rear, beyond grey wastegrounds, reared up the skeletal headgear of Chatterley Whitfield Colliery. One of the most successful pits in the North Staffordshire coalfield, they'd tried to turn it into a museum on closure, but it didn't work out, not enough tourists interested in going underground, too much like hard work. There's a surprise!

I shed crocodile tears for the lost industry and caught a 99B to Tunstall, encountering en route, Pittshill Victory Working Men's Club – CIU Affiliated. We were in Tunstall before I knew it. I was decanted in Tower Square and walked over to admire its Clock Tower, 'erected by public subscription in 1893 to mark the 86th birthday of Sir Smith Child, Bart, a philanthropist'. How nice to be so remembered. A florist was doing what appeared to be good business by the tower, and smokers were downing pints and drawing assiduously on their cigarettes outside the Oddfellows Arms. I looked back down at the Town Hall, which morphs into the Market Hall. Emblazoned on the façade I read the words PEACE HAPPINESS TRUTH JUSTICE and I trusted that Tunstall's inhabitants made every attempt to live up to these virtues on a daily basis.

Northernmost of the blurred and amorphous Six Towns, Tunstall had finally fallen into sharper focus for me on reading Paul Johnson's charming memoir *The Vanished Landscape*, which evokes a simpler, and perhaps happier world that existed here between the two world wars. Johnson's family home overlooked Victoria Park, to which I swiftly made tracks, anxiously glancing at the Clock Tower in recognition that the afternoon was marching on apace, and I still had two more towns to attend to.

A side street at the north end of the Town Hall led me past the Silver Coin arcade, the premises of Dream Wools, and Age Concern (closed down!) to a subway leading to the library, housed in the Jubilee Buildings of 1889, where also are to be found the municipal baths: books and bathing; unusual bedfellows. On the way to Queen's Avenue – where, as a boy, Paul Johnson lived at 'Park View' – I crossed the Loop Line, or rather, I crossed the public right of way where the Loop Line railway used to run before Beeching and Marples conspired to close it down in 1964. Something of a misnomer, they call it the Greenway now, though I suppose it provides an energetic means of walking, or cycling or jogging between Kidsgrove, Tunstall, Burslem and Hanley without encountering any death-threatening road traffic; drug-dealers

Chatterley Whitfield from Fegg Hayes

being another matter. But I couldn't help wondering what transportation benefits might have accrued if it had been modernised into a rapid-transit, inter-urban highway as opposed to just being abandoned. Johnson and his sisters travelled to school on the Loop Line and adored its bowler-hatted stationmasters, parcels offices, waiting rooms, enamel advertisements and platform trolleys bearing milk churns: 'My sisters and I loved this railway. It was 'ours',' he recalls vividly in his memoir. Tunstall station ('cavernous, smoke-stained and fumigerous') was reached down a steep track. The void where it stood still is but now there is merely open grassland and a rusty old signal, cosmetically retained, plaintively awaiting ghost trains.

Along with the railway station, another symbolic feature in Paul Johnson's early life was the Roman Catholic Church of the Sacred Heart. In fact he lived just two doors down, one house away from the presbytery. The church was barely older than the boy, having been completed in 1930. It was the brainchild of an ambitious priest, Father Ryan, who had badgered and bullied its architect, J. S. Brocklesby, to such an extent that the professional renounced his commission, leaving the priest to finish off the design (with the help of Heavenly voices, perhaps) himself. The result, with its three and a half copper domes, is both Gothic and Baroque at the same time, with a little bit of Romanesque thrown in for good measure. 'A piece of artistic nonsense', was what Paul Johnson's father called it. And he should know, for he was head of Burslem Art School, and a friend of L. S. Lowry.

I would dearly liked to have seen inside the church,

Tunstall market place

What's left of the Loop Line

to see how it compared to Pugin's work at Cheadle, but even the outer gates were padlocked. So I walked across the road and went to watch the locals playing bowls instead, which, as activities go, was probably just as good for their souls. Tunstall (or Victoria) Park was the young Paul Johnson's own personal adventure playground. 'I was in it every day, often (as I grew older) all day'. Along with Town Halls, parks were something dear to the council officials of the Six Towns. Even lowly Fenton has a fine example. I just wish they still had boats for hire on the boating lakes. Otherwise I imagine the park would still be recognisable to Paul Johnson, seventy years on. However, I did doubt if the all-pervading aroma of curry being prepared in neighbouring houses would have been present in the 1930s.

I couldn't resist a peep at what they now call 'Tunstall Pool' on the way back, Victorian swimming baths are an endangered species in the age of the ubiquitous leisure centre. Paul Johnson relates an amusing story of how his sisters dressed him as a girl to facilitate swimming lessons at a time when the sexes were still strictly segregated. He had been marched up the street in an old dress, stockings and a beret under the assumed name of 'Polly' and would have seen the deceit through but for a nosy little neighbour called Cynthia. Fortunately she was bribed off, having broken the rule of not wearing lifebelts in the shallow end.

The ancient facility took me back to my own childhood, but I have an embarrassing tale to relate too. No-one prevented me from sneaking in and climbing the stairs to the spectators gallery. But no sooner had I opened the swing door, and was looking down in awe at the old-fashioned pool lined with changing cubicles, than a young life guard apprehended me.

'Are you alright there?' he asked cagily. 'We're not open to the public just now, it's schools only.'

Suddenly, horrifyingly, the penny dropped. I was being taken for voyeur at best, but in all probability, much worse, a paedophile.

In retrospect I'm surprised the viewing gallery isn't permanently barred and bolted. Sheepishly I mumbled something innocuous about just wanting to see the old pool, but I could still sense I was being judged guilty until proven innocent, and beat a hasty retreat as soon as I decently could.

I took a No.21 to Burslem and sat opposite a man in exotic dress and headgear which made me think he must have come from Afghanistan, but he was probably just from Longport. Wherever he hailed from, he looker cooler than the rest of us.

'When are they going to get air-conditioning on these buses?' observed the woman in the seat behind me out loud. The rest of us assumed her enquiry was of a rhetorical nature, and no-one bothered to provide an answer.

I was reminded of the equally warm opening of *Anna of the Five Towns*, and idly wondered if our habit of wearing scantier clothing these days rendered us more susceptible to heat, rather than less.

We dropped out of Tunstall past the inevitable retail park. How long before Tunstall is renamed 'Asdaley'; Stoke, 'Sainsburyton'; and Longton, 'Tescoville'?

As the domes of the Sacred Heart diminished over my shoulder, the floodlights and grandstands of Port Vale Football Club took over responsibility for being the landscape's dominant feature. We stopped to let a gaggle of young people board, uniformly attired in City of Stoke-on-Trent sweatshirts. They'd been to the Dimensions Leisure Centre and were in high spirits, before, that is, they saw that the bus was full and they'd need to stand. In collective dismay they chorused an expletive that appeared to my delicate ears to rhyme with Luke again.

'When are they going to put more buses on this route?' asked the rhetorical philosopher behind me. And again no reply was forthcoming from the perspiring throng.

The road breasted a rise by the Royal Stafford Pottery and the bus began to roll down into Burslem. I alighted at Swan Bank, or rather 'Duck Bank' as Bennett called it. For my sojourn in Burslem I proposed to entertain myself by following the 'Bursley Trail', a self-guided walk around some of the key locations in his Five Towns novels and short stories.

Somewhat out of character, I began at the beginning, an imposing 18th Century house on the corner of Wedgwood Street and Moorland Road. In *Clayhanger* it features as the Conservative Club, in reality it was once the home of two of Josiah Wedgwood's uncles, Thomas and John. Now it houses a company of Independent Financial Advisors, an occupation we might all do well to aspire to in these straightened times.

The trail led up Wedgwood Street past the site of the butchers' market (or Shambles) referred to in *The Old Wives' Tale* and on with the Queen's Theatre (Burslem's *third* Town Hall) on my right to where the Blood Tub, or Snagg's Theatre had stood. On the way up I saw that the former Post Office had been converted into a small art gallery. The Queen's Theatre was prominently advertising the appearance of 'The Ultimate Sixties Band' (plus comedian and vocalist). It was unclear as to whether the band were

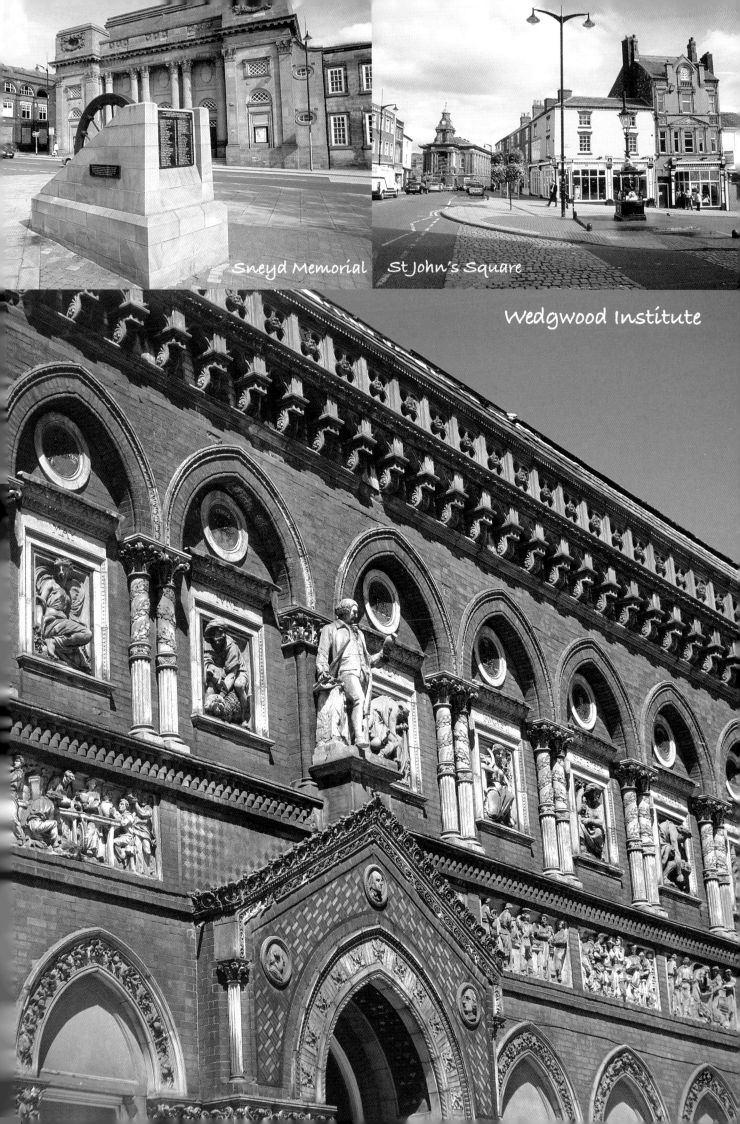

Sneyd Memorial   St John's Square

Wedgwood Institute

sexagenarians or that their repertoire hailed from the 'sixties. Then I realised that was probably one and the same thing. Across the road from the theatre a memorial commemorates the fifty-seven victims of an explosion at Sneyd Colliery in 1942, their ages ranging from fifteen to sixty-five.

Burslem's second Town Hall – the one with the golden angel perched on top – was the next point of call. I found myself chuckling at the thought of Denry Machin inviting himself to a ball within and having the effrontery to ask the Countess of Chell to dance with him in *The Card*. It now rather self-effacingly houses an exhibition called Ceramica.

The trail continued into St John's Square, or St Luke's Square as Bennett would have it. On the corner, opposite an elaborate cast iron fountain, some premises were in the process of being opened up as Denry's Bar, Hotel and Restaurant. Bennett would have been tickled. For my part I was rather put out that the Bull's Head, brewery tap for Titanic Ales, was shut to the world, for I felt like sinking a pint, never mind a luxury liner.

Now for Burslem's *pièce de résistance*, the Wedgwood Institute, a Venetian Gothic confection of red brick and terracotta complete with a statue of Josiah Wedgwood surmounting the entrance and a sequence of sculpted tableaux depicting the signs of the zodiac, the months of the year, and the processes involved in the manufacture of pottery. Gladstone laid the foundation stone in 1863, and the building opened for business six years later. Rudyard Kipling's father, John Lockwood Kipling, was one of the designers involved before he emigrated to India. It reminded me of an elaborate chocolate cake. In a more fashionable location it would be hugely honoured.

The last time I'd been in town it housed the Library. Now (naturally – there is nothing as certain in life as death, taxes, and the continual re-location of tourist information centres and libraries) that had been moved, if only across the street into the former Art School (where Paul Johnson's father once worked, you'll recall), an erection of 1905 not without its own stylishness. As for the Institute, it is apparently in need of restoration and, in the jargon of the Burslem Regeneration Company, 'an economically sustainable new use'. I was further worried to learn that the same organisation believe that the best solution to revitalise the town is to attract one of the major supermarkets. Morrisons – absent from the list I suggested back at Tunstall – seems the obvious answer, and 'Morrisonby' rolls off the tongue quite easily, doesn't it?

I completed my perambulation in Swan Square, alias Duck Square, which is a more accurate indicator of its architectural impact. Here stand the premises which Bennett imagined contained the Clayhanger Steam Printing Works. Nowadays they are painted a garish blue and provide a home to a Lettings Agency. Close by, at the Queen's Head, afternoon drinkers were singing raucously along to the Four Tops, 'standing in the shadows of love, getting ready for the heartaches to come'. I hoped, against my better judgement, that the lyrics didn't prove prophetic where the regeneration of the Mother Town of the Potteries was concerned.

Back at the bus stop stood a man with a clip-board.

'And would you like to add any other comments?' he was saying to the shelter's only other occupant, a woman of early middle age.

'Well, the drivers could be a bit more happier,' she replied. 'Especially them Eastern Europeans … Poles and what nots. Mind you, having said that,' she continued, 'I don't use the buses as much as I used to. I walk a lot now.'

Arnold Bennett called Waterloo Road 'Trafalgar Road'. Here ran the steam trams up to the fashionable suburb of 'Bleakridge': Cobridge in what passes for reality hereabouts. I wished I was on a steam tram, rather than one of First's ubiquitous single-deckers. A PMT Leyland Tiger would have been a marked improvement. I rather wished I was sitting between Janet Orgreave and Hilda Lessways, contemplating a convivial soirée at Lane End House.

Bennett lived on Waterloo Road himself, at No.205. I was embarrassed on his behalf. Waterloo Road is not the gilded thoroughfare it once was. The well-to-do upped sticks long ago, and their once elegant homes provide dreary accommodation for transients. No.205 itself was 'To Let', and to Stoke-on-Trent's collective shame there wasn't even a plaque to draw attention to the great man's occupancy.

School was coming out as we passed St Peter's Roman Catholic Church and its presbytery. Given the colour and the clothing of the waiting parents it might have been Mumbai. I couldn't imagine for the life of me that Bennett could have foreseen such a transition, though he may have found good copy in the changing scene. A mobile phone rang loudly to a salsa rhythm. The vehicle's occupants looked about them in astonishment, wondering at the nature of the individual outgoing enough to chose such a tune. It was a plump and elderly lady, who, in answering it loudly, evinced not a shadow of shame.

Hanley again! Threading a maze of side streets we came to the bus station, vouchsafed en route a glimpse of the French-looking Town Hall, built as an hotel in 1867. I was beginning to lose count of the number of Town Halls, past and present, encountered thus far. It takes some time to fathom Hanley's street pattern, probably because there *is* no pattern. For all its chain stores and facilities, architecturally it underwhelms, a limitation which adds curious piquancy to the whole sorry business of the evasive City of Stoke-on-Trent. This is not to say I don't like the Six Towns. On the contrary, I admire them immensely – their contradictions, their uncertainties, their ludicrous affiliation, and soon after making this journey I was appalled to learn that the Stoke-on-Trent City Partnership were seriously proposing to play down the name Hanley in favour of 'City Centre'. 'We've got to function as a city ,' they cried. 'It's about investment and regeneration.' Chums, you are missing the point, barking up the wrong tree, or simply barking mad. The unique synergies and juxtapositions of the Six Towns should be enhanced and celebrated, fêted far and wide, not kept secret, like an embarrassing family trait.

I couldn't find Fenton anywhere on the departure boards, but enquiries led me to Bay 8, where Service No.6 for Meir Park or 6A for Blythe Bridge promised to land me at this most elusive, and least prepossessing of the Six Towns. Purportedly operating at ten minute intervals, neither service made an appearance. Other buses to other destinations arrived and departed with increasingly irritating regularity. A lengthy queue built up. The sky assumed the colour of a ripening

bruise. Somewhere off-stage there were Wagnerian peels of thunder. With a bit of practice, the waiting throng might have put on a passable performance of Havergal Brian's *Gothic Symphony*. Certainly there were enough of us, all wanting to get to Fenton, for reasons best known to ourselves.

Eventually, of course, a No.6 sidled sheepishly in. Employing my elbows to good effect, I forced my way to the front of the queue. Then they decided to swap drivers. Following that it began to rain. Rather than retreat back under the canopy in an undignified manner, I chose to remain where I was, while the new driver went through his bags of change as methodically as a trainee accountant. When, in the fullness of bus company time, I was permitted to board, I derived some satisfaction in the pulp-like nature of my paper ticket, which I had clutched resolutely in my hand as the deluge descended.

We could have filled two buses or, perish the thought, a double-decker. I offered my seat to a svelte blonde with a stud in her nose. She appeared nonplussed at such throwback manners, and graciously demurred. She was no substitute for Helen (With the High Hand) Rathbone.

'They ought to have more buses on this route,' cried a familiar voice behind me. I didn't dare turn to look. Progress was desultory in the burgeoning tea-time traffic. We crawled past the Bridgewater Pottery and over the Caldon Canal. A narrowboat would have made swifter progress. We crawled on, stuttering

War Memorial, Fenton

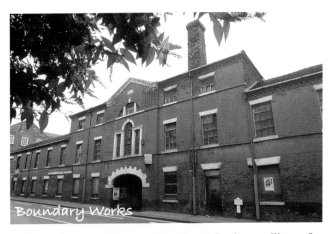
Boundary Works

and starting past Ravensdale Retail Park, a gallimaufry of well known names: Aldi, Netto, McDonalds and Gala Bingo. Was that the strippling Trent we were crossing over, or the Styx?

Fenton Domestics, read a shop sign, and I leapt to the not unreasonable conclusion that I must be nearing my goal. Fenton Fryer and Fenton Baptist Church seemed to confirm my suspicions. I fought my way off the crowded bus. It growled away in a blue cloud of diesel fumes. When the smoke cleared I saw that I was in a nondescript street of little shops. I was baffled, perplexed. I could recall seeing photographs of a Town Hall and an imposing parish church. There was nothing in sight above the ambition of two storeys. I pressed on, but could tell that the shops were petering out. Instinct made me turn right at a roundabout. On the corner, a French restaurant and bistro called Bonaparte's had been abandoned, obviously the *entente* hadn't been *cordiale* enough for it to make a go of things. I progressed to Fenton Health Centre, whose facilities I almost needed as I leapt out of the determined path of a cyclist on the pavement.

A sign pointing to the Magistrates Court looked promising. Across the road stood a lovely trio of

Phoenix Works

bottle kilns. And then a library! And even though it was closed on Wednesday afternoons, the sheer dignity of its architecture was reassuring. Could I be on the brink of the real Fenton? Was that the thumping I could hear of its municipal heart? Yes,

yes, yes. Fenton was *not* a figment of *my* imagination; even if it had failed to fire Arnold Bennett's. For now I was in Albert Square, facing a poignant war memorial, with the Town Hall beyond, and Christ Church to the side. If I had lighted on the Lost City of the Aztecs, I couldn't have been more excited. And what matter that, the other two sides of the square were an insubstantial afterthought of council flats and red brick walling.

I wandered into a little art gallery to celebrate, hoping that they might sell postcards. They didn't but they promised to think about it. I bought an ice cream instead and went off in search of a bus stop. All that remained now was to get back to Longton.

Have you ever played that game that you play with bus stops? You know the one, where you wait for a while, then decide to walk to the next one, only the bus passes you half way. That's the game I played between Fenton and Longton. Buses 6 –Author 0.

Longton Town Hall

Thus it came to pass that the last leg of my journey was performed quite literally on my last legs. The Department for Health are working on a poster campaign as I write. Still, it enabled me to savour some nuances that might have been lost aboard a bus: an elegant row of stucco houses at Foley Place; the Boundary Works of 1819; and the Phoenix Works of 1881.

And so I staggered into the second most famous Times Square in the world, the effect of Longton's noble Town Hall diminished somewhat by railway girders. Totting up the miles I'd travelled resulted in a paltry maximum of twenty. It goes without saying that it had seemed much more. Not so much six towns, more six continents. I wondered how the Germans were getting on in the Lake District. They had travelled much further, but perhaps not quite so far.

Walking Backwards 2

Acouple of days later found me alighting at Codsall station, poised to embark on the next stage of my Staffordshire Way walk which would take me to Cannock Chase, some eighteen miles away. It goes without saying that the station pub was closed: Wetherspoons apart, even so-called 'all-day' pubs haven't opened their doors by nine-thirty in the morning. But what a pretty little station Codsall is! It's almost as authentic a Great Western Railway stop as you'll find on the Severn Valley Railway. All that was missing was the milk churns. Suffice it to say, it put me in a good frame of mind and I strode along Station Road – past the War Memorial – looking optimistically forward to the blank canvas of the day ahead.

Codsall is the headquarters of South Staffordshire, a district which emerged from the regional boundary changes of the mid 1970s. At that time a chunk of what had long been Staffordshire was subsumed within the nebulous new county called West Midlands, leaving South Staffordshire to hang pendulously down from the rest of the county like a ... well I won't go into detail ... let's just say it brought to mind the bull I'd met on my previous walk. The West Midlands annexed Staffordshire's Black Country, running off with its booty, the alliterative towns of Wolverhampton, Walsall, West Bromwich, Willenhall and Wednesbury.

But I wasn't about to be side-tracked by political angst that bright morning, and I found myself quite liking Codsall. Apart from anything else, its surprising array of facilities – shops, pubs, banks and all the other paraphernalia of 21st Century civilisation – make it a more than useful staging post for toilers on the Staffordshire Way. In the window of Flappers Tea Shop I caught sight of a picture of Codsall station. It was post card size so I went in to see if they had any for sale.

'Yes, it is a post card,' confirmed the lady behind the counter. 'I'll just see if there's any left.'

As she rummaged in a box on a nearby shelf she filled me in on a local point of detail: 'Of course that's not the original footbridge you see today,' she explained. 'That's a replica! The one on the post card is the original timber bridge. The new one's metal.'

'Well it fooled me,' I laughed. 'I was thinking how pretty the station looked when I got off the train.'

'It's Italianate, you know,' she continued, finally locating a bundle of cards. 'Edward Banks, the Wolverhampton architect designed it. It's a bit of local history.'

'And we all need as much local history as we can get,' I quipped as money changed hands and the transaction was completed.

Outside again, I paused to look at a statue of 'The Lone Singer', sculpted by Sir Charles Wheeler and bequeathed to the parish of his birth. Wheeler studied at Wolverhampton College of Art and later the Royal College of Art. In 1956, he became the first sculptor to be elected President of the Royal Academy. Amongst his greatest works were the massive (40 tons each of Portland stone) figures Earth and Water for the Ministry of Defence headquarters in Whitehall. Apparently Air and Fire were victims of an armed forces budget cut!

Church Road led me out of Codsall, through a quiet enclave of bay-windowed semis, hydrangea borders and cooing pigeons. There were comic London overtones to be encountered at Hyde Park Cottage and Drury Lane. Behind a hedge on Gunstone Lane a woman was calling persistently 'in', but whatever or whoever she was addressing – an errant husband perhaps – it or they appeared reluctant to co-operate.

I left the security of tarmac astern at New House Farm and took to a succession of field paths. Moat Brook was flagged up ahead by the inevitable belt of balsam. I passed a pond noisy with geese. I could smell Gunstone Hall Riding Centre before I saw it. An elderly couple dressed for serious walking came round the corner holding hands and symmetrically arranged so that one had a walking pole in their left hand and the other one in their right hand. Time had joined them at the hip, a matrimonial merging

Chillington Hall

of body and soul. They even bid me 'good morning' in chorus.

In my possession was an Ordnance Survey one inch map for Wolverhampton dated 1921. Linen-backed, it had stood the test of time rather better than the landscape it depicted. I saw myself as the pipe-smoking, cloth-capped, Norfolk-jacketed cyclist illustrated by Ellis Martin on the cover. Had I been him I would have been spared the intrusion of the M54 motorway, whose incessant traffic noise had been gathering to a crescendo since leaving Codsall. The motorways have made England a smaller place and I begrudge them that. Saving time seems to me a futile pursuit, especially as much of what we think we've 'saved' is frittered away unrewardingly. I have no doubt that it is better to spend a day walking twenty miles than driving five hundred.

As the traffic's roar thankfully diminished, I decided to leave the Staffordshire Way so as to gain a closer view of Chillington Hall. It was only a minor detour that I had in mind, but it questioned the logic of the Way's routeing to the east. I was smugly pleased with my small desertion, because the hall came into view almost immediately. A lengthy picket fence kept members of the *hoi polloi*, such as me, in our proper place on the public road. Within, gracious parkland, laid out by Capability Brown and peppered by stately chestnut trees – both sweet and horse – stretched into a privileged, landowning infinity. How

Chillington's Longhorns

splendidly the east façade's pedimented portico stamped its personality on the hall. All that history under one sprawling roof. It was beyond comprehension, like outer space. Catholics and Royalists, the Giffards came over with William the Conqueror. One of them aided King Charles II in his escape after the Battle of Worcester. Had it been past two o'clock on a selected afternoon in the summer months, I might have parted with some money, gone inside, and gazed about me with appropriate awe, but it wasn't even yet eleven and I had many miles to cover.

Turning my back on the house, I set off along the unclassified road which runs parallel to Chillington's private drive or ride. A picturesque herd of longhorn cattle lay recumbent in the shadows cast by the wide avenue of trees, flicking flies off their mottled flanks with their tails. Soon I was back on the Staffordshire Way, crossing the ride, and finding my way past Woolley Farm to the village of Brewood. I have been familiar with 'Brood', as the locals call it, for thirty years, but always from the perspective of the Shropshire Union Canal. It was a pleasant novelty for me to approach it differently. For a start I'd never noticed a cream-washed Arts & Crafts house called The Mount before, yet there it stands, not even a hundred yards from the canal at Bridge 12. Crossing the bridge, and following the path on its approach to the centre of the village, I

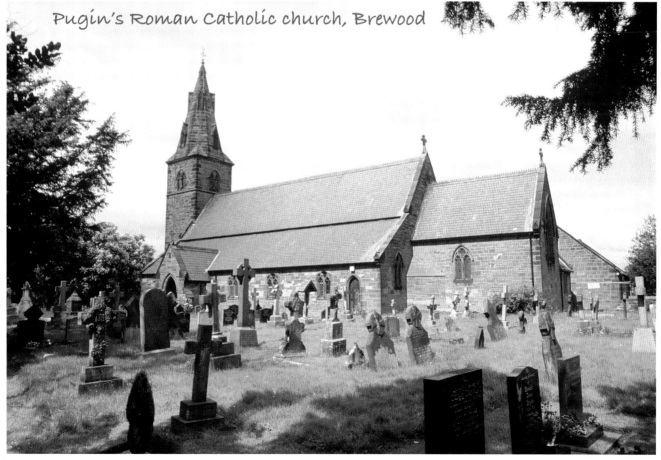

Pugin's Roman Catholic church, Brewood

was further enlightened by a side-on view of one of the canal's characterising embankments, a view most boaters miss. Then, as if to complete the illusion that I was visiting somewhere for the first time, I squeezed my way along a snicket which led into the street opposite the church, almost tempted to pick a handful of fruit from the damson tree hanging invitingly over the alleyway.

In a contradictory kind of way, Brewood has benefited from lying off the Watling Street and never having been connected to the railway system. My old friend Mike Webb, who was born and raised in the village and attended its former grammar school, used to tell me that the boys in Brewood happily collected boat names as opposed to engine numbers. Brewood remained off the beaten track until the last quarter of the 20th Century by which time the flexibility offered by road transport turned it into a burgeoning dormitory for Wolverhampton. Busier perhaps now than it has ever been, its discreet and mellow architecture remains its saving grace. Its streets curve alluringly towards the old market place, it boasts two fine churches, a convent school for girls, and an extraordinary Gothick concoction called Speedwell Castle, a mid 18th Century town house with prominent ogee windows like arched eyebrows erected with the winnings on a race horse called Speedwell.

I sat gazing at Speedwell Castle's exquisite fenestration whilst waiting for the mushroom omelette I'd ordered for what amounted to an early lunch (even by my standards!) at The Mess, a café by day and bistro by night. I was beginning to regret choosing an outdoor table, for the market place was being rendered noisy by a raucous gang of scaffolders on the roof of the neighbouring Lion Hotel. Their vehicles littered the square to such an extent that through traffic frequently came to a standstill. Still, it was nice to see a considerable contingent of agricultural appliances mixed up with the ubiquitous vans and cars, and it was good to see that the Green Bus Company still operated hourly to Wolverhampton, even if they appeared to have Arriva as a rival now.

After I'd eaten, I set off along Bargate Street, noting St Dominic's school which still had the look about it of the workhouse it had originally been. I was tickled by the petrol pumps at High Green Garage and the rare legend in these times: 'We Serve You'! Pausing only briefly to take a snap shot of Pugin's little Roman Catholic church, I rejoined the canal by the Bridge Inn, noting that the height of the structure it derived its name from emphasised the sheer depth of Telford's canal cutting at this point. I broke into a lengthy stride along the towpath, emulating the way that the Shropshire Union (formerly the Birmingham & Liverpool Junction Canal) appears to lope across the landscape. Boats were moored up for lunch; each, according to the taste and prosperity of its owner, a microcosm of human life.

Telford's Stretton Aqueduct

There's something felicitous in the numbering of canal bridges – you know, quite literally, where you are with them. By Bridge 16 I could see Broom Hall, once the home of William Carless, who famously hid King Charles II in an oak tree at Boscobel just over the border in Shropshire. Further views were then swallowed up by a shallow cutting, at the far end of which the feeder from Belvide Reservoir came gurgling into the canal.

When, as a gauche twenty-something working for *Waterways World* magazine in the early 'eighties, I first wrote about Stretton Aqueduct, which carries the canal across the A5, I blithely followed a number of printed sources in erroneously attributing both the canal and the road to Telford, later discovering to my embarrassment, that Telford's road to Holyhead had proceeded on quite a different course between Daventry and Wellington. It was a useful moral for a nascent guide book compiler to learn: always cross-reference your sources!

Following the canal towpath allows more time to take in the aqueduct than the motorist, hurrying below, is allowed. More time to take it in, to note the beauty of its curved stonework, the inlaid brick, its elegant wrought iron railings. I stood and watched a boat pass over it, chugging along at a measured pace unlike the roaring traffic below. I wished I could turn back the clock to the date of the aqueducts's completion in 1832, and watch horse-drawn carts rumbling below in place of the relentless traffic of the present day.

North of Stretton Aqueduct, the canal enters Lapley Wood Cutting, so wooded now that it almost forms an emerald tunnel. Engaging my brain in a lateral gear, it occurred to me that all these trees wouldn't have been here when Telford's navvies cut this deep gash through the landscape. And then I wondered if the trees had been deliberately planted as a windbreak, but they didn't appear regimented enough for that, so I just assumed they had grown up over a century and a half, one seeding the next until the dense jungle-like vegetation encountered now was formed.

Halfway through the cutting I came upon a canal milepost informing me that I was 7 miles from Autherley Junction (on the outskirts of Wolverhampton) and 32 from Nantwich, the B&LJ's northern terminus. However, I wouldn't be seeing the next milepost, because the Staffordshire Way leaves the towpath at Bridge 17. Lowing cattle hinted that I was about to pass through a farmyard. A metal gate made a din that its wooden predecessor would have considered impolite. One of the extensive outbuildings bore the inscription 'ES 1889'. I like structures to be

date-stamped. The farmhouse itself was substantial and approached by a curving gravel drive, seemingly the dwelling of a gentleman farmer and no mere tenant. Further down the lane I came upon a pair of high-gabled farmworkers' cottages, markedly more modest in design.

The sturdy tower of Lapley church appeared ahead of me. According to the map I was about to cross a Roman Road running in a north-westerly direction from the Watling Street, perhaps with a view to reaching Chester. The aroma of fresh mown grass reached me from the churchyard, through which the Staffordshire Way is pleasingly routed. All Saints church was disappointingly locked, but I perused the graveyard, discovering some plaintive inscriptions, such as the raised tomb in memory of John Howie Healey who died on the 24th February 1824 aged 10 weeks. A tall and elegant memorial to various members of the Bickford family also made melancholy reading: William Bickford of Paradise (his home or his destination?) died on the 11th July 1896 aged 55 years; his wife, Emma Susan, died a fortnight later, aged 58 years; their daughter, Annie Eliza, died on the 25th November 1898 aged 28.

Long ago there was a priory at Lapley occupied by the black-habited monks of the Benedictine order. They hailed originally from Rheims in France where the third son of Alfgar, Lord of the Manor at the beginning of the 11th Century, had died on the way back from a pilgrimage to Rome. Alfgar honoured his son's deathbed wish to provide lands for the Benedictines. Virtually nothing remains of the priory but the Staffordshire Way traverses a meadow in which a deep depression recalls the existence of a moat. Glancing back over my shoulder I caught sight of The Wrekin.

Then it was out into lonely countryside again. A wheat field gave way to polytunnels filled with strawberry plants. I almost transgressed the Eighth Commandment. At Longnor Mill Farm Friesian cattle were keeping cool beneath a corrugated iron awning.

Bickford Meadows

Penkridge. On the top of Cannock Chase the telecommunications tower didn't appear to get any nearer. I began to wish I'd followed my instinct as opposed to the waymarkers and gone via Whiston and Cuttlestone Bridge.

A cup of tea and slab of cake at the Dickens of a Tea Shoppe in Penkridge went some way to restoring me. In common with Brewood, Penkridge is somewhere I've long been familiar with on account of my canal travels. I have seen its fortunes ebb and flow from one economic cycle to the next. Culturally it can point to its imposing collegiate church; Brindley's Staffordshire & Worcestershire Canal, which curves picturesquely past the town; several old coaching inns; and Joseph Locke's Grand Junction Railway viaduct. Commercially it can point to its popular outdoor market. Yet I still sensed that Penkridge could do with a good old-fashioned tonic of one sort or another.

Wishing it luck in that respect, I sought out the towpath and set off in a northerly direction. Belonging to an earlier generation of canal building, the Staffs & Worcs contrasts quaintly with the Shropshire Union. It contrasts even more quaintly with the M6

Mitton Massey

The Way turned east along the banks of Whiston Brook, a headwater of the River Penk. In the sky what at first I took to be a light aircraft circling, turned out to be a remote controlled model. Bickford Meadows Nature Reserve is managed by the Staffordshire Wildlife Trust who bill it as 'an oasis in an agricultural desert'. I wished I'd had a better informed companion with me to identify such native plants as ragged robin, brooklime and common spotted orchid. I wished I could have distinguished whitethroats and chiffchaffs amidst the birdsong. Neither did I encounter any otters, owls, stoats, weasels, frogs, toads or voles, but they were there, watching me for sure, I could feel it in my bones.

At Mitton a gang of old boys on bikes pedalled garrulously past me, dressed in colouful lycra as if they were taking part in the Tour de France, which, conceivably they were … in their imagination. Crossing Church Eaton Brook, I followed the waymarkers along metalled lancs for just over half a mile before the Way kicked back on itself, dog-leg fashion, and plunged along the overgrown perimeter of an as yet unharvested oilseed rape crop. After Preston Vale Farm it was something of a trek into

58

motorway which parallels the canal out of Penkridge. I kept pace with two boats until they encountered respective locks. The bridges on this canal carry not only numbers, but names as well. Teddesley Park Bridge was built in an ornamental style because it carried the coach road to Teddesley Hall, the seat of Sir Edward Littleton, one of the chief promoters of the canal. The hall was demolished after the Second World War, having been used as a prison camp for German officers.

The Staffordshire Way leaves the canal at Park Gate Lock and heads in a north-easterly direction for Cannock Chase. I found myself climbing through a

The Glacial Boulder

field of clover with a hot sun beating down on my neck. The next field, depicted on the map as being part of the Teddesley estate's parkland, turned out to be a wheat field with no discernible path through it. Had it not been liberally coated in duckweed I might well have hurled myself into the neighbouring pond. I plodded on under the sky's hostile glare, grateful at last to reach the Wellington Belt, a linear wood planted to commemorate a visit to Teddesley Hall by the Iron Duke. It was reinvigoratingly cool in the wood and jays were calling to each other. A railway sleeper bridge carried me over a brook followed by a sleeper causeway over boggy ground. This would have been a particularly pleasant interlude were it not for encroaching nettles.

'With unemployment going through the roof, why can't people be paid to maintain public rights of way?' I wondered aloud. But then perhaps the Staffordshire Way isn't regarded as a priority. After all the most recent guide published to it dates back to 1996, and, not having found it in any local bookshops, I had to go to the council office in Stafford to obtain a copy. Furthermore, I hadn't met

another walker since before Brewood, which doesn't exactly suggest that the route is a popular one with ramblers. Escaping from the nettles' grasp, I found myself having to trudge across a field of stubble.

From Gypsy Green, I followed Cock Lane, rustic, wide-verged and metalled. It brought me subconsciously to Bednal. On the far side of the village I nodded to a cheerful little chap gardening with a cigar sticking out of the corner of his mouth. I could read his mind, it was saying: 'Why bother with this rambling lark when you can stay put in your own garden puffing at a cigar.' At that moment I couldn't have given him a convincing answer.

Beyond the A34 I began to ascend the shoulders of Cannock Chase. A trio of buzzards were riding the thermals and crying out to each other in sheer delight. A fundamental change overcame the landscape. All attempts at agriculture were futile. I climbed Sycamores Hill and then descended into the Oldacre Valley. A First World War army camp had stood hereabouts, though there was scant trace of its former existence. There were, however, traces of animal presence in the shape of a variety of droppings: fox? badger? deer? unluckily I was no expert. Some 650 feet above sea level I came to the conclusion of the day's march at the Glacial Boulder, a bit of litter carelessly left behind by a melting glacier at the end of the Ice Age. It wasn't the only litter. All along the widened verge where cars are parked lay evidence of the human race's baser proclivities. Sex and hamburgers, that about sums us up!

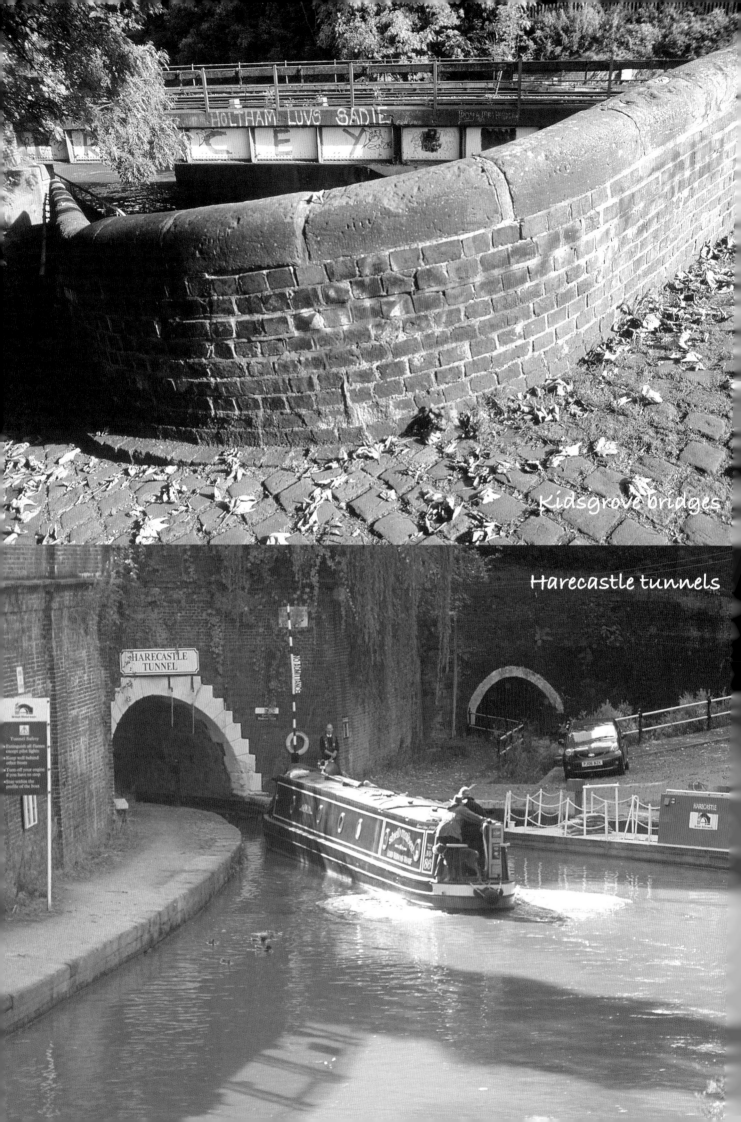

Kidsgrove bridges

Harecastle tunnels

Big Tunnel
Little Tunnel

*I*N a week in which a seventeen year old had completed a solo circumnavigation of the world, it seemed thoroughly appropriate that I should emulate his feat by boating from Kidsgrove to Leek in a single day. But there the comparisons ran out, there would be minor differences: I would be travelling seventeen miles, not thirty thousand; I would not (I trusted) have to contend with fifty foot waves; I was three times (and a bit) his age; and I had an accomplice. The accomplice and I limbered up for the challenge ahead with cheese and bacon oatcakes from Brenda's. We were both sportsmen and recognised the importance of a high calorie intake. Rob needed three thousand a day just to stay slim. I needed three thousand a day just to stay … well let's get on with the story.

There was consternation at the mouth of Harecastle Tunnel. There had been a breach on the Shropshire Union which had had the knock-on effect of routeing more boaters via the Trent & Mersey.

'We've had three hundred and sixty boats through in four days,' said Derek, the tunnel-keeper, mopping his brow. 'That's well up! I came down the other morning and got the shock of my life. Boats were stretching as far as the eye could see. That's when I knew there was something up! I went and counted them, then I rang through to Dave at the other end. "Dave, I've got sixteen boats here waiting to come through." He couldn't believe it. Then we got to know about the Shebdon Breach …'

It was difficult not to be thrilled by the way Derek said 'Shebdon Breach', it gave it the gravitas of a great natural disaster, up there with Vesuvius and the Johnstown Flood.

But Derek hadn't delivered his punchline:

'They've had to go to Portugal for the clay. There's no marl round here now, what with all the potteries closing down. It could take weeks!'

Rob and I counted ourselves as fortunate, that *Deli* was one of only two boats waiting to be the first through Harecastle from the north that morning. *Deli* is Rob's pride and joy, a thirty-eight foot narrow boat. He had been its owner for six months and had renamed it in memory of the black labrador he'd grown up with.

Taking a boat through Harecastle Tunnel is one of the great inland waterway adventures. I know this because I read it in the guide book I wrote twenty-eight years ago. I could regurgitate all the facts contained therein, but that might stop you rushing out to buy the current edition of *Pearson's Canal Companion to the Four Counties Ring*, so I won't. Suffice it to say, that Harecastle Tunnel is one and three-quarter miles long and it took us a creditable thirty-seven minutes to pass through, and that the inside was drier than I remembered it, a good many canal tunnels featuring mini-Niagara-like torrents within. Seasoned boat crews put up their umbrellas on entering a tunnel.

In cargo-carrying days electric tugs hauled boats through Harecastle to avoid a build-up of engine fumes. They dragged themselves along a steel cable laid on the canal bed, collecting power from an overhead cable through a tram-like pole. Nowadays a system of forced ventilation is employed, fumes being sucked out by a gigantic fan at the south end of the tunnel. It can be a bit unnerving to see the slowly widening circle of light at the south end suddenly cut off as the ventilation doors clang shut, and the suction fans begin their ghostly roar. Unnerving, that is, for the amateur.

It had been overcast in Kidsgrove – though I have it on good authority that cloud isn't a permanent feature of the climate there … well, pretty good authority, the Kidsgrove Tourist Board – but we emerged from the southern portal of Harecastle into a halo of brilliant sunshine and a welcoming committee of Canada geese, or 'Canads' as Rob called them. Dave stood waiting with his clip-board to record our exit, the authorities are averse to losing boats in mid-tunnel. Innumerate, I lost count of the number of boats waiting to go in.

The Trent & Mersey Canal which weaves its post-industrial way along the foot of the ridge on which Tunstall, Burslem and Hanley stand is unrecognisable from the one described so atmospherically in the opening pages of *Clayhanger*. In truth it's changed out of all recognition in the thirty years I've been familiar with it. Rob was too young to remember the National Garden Festival of 1986, let alone when Shelton Bar had its own blast furnaces. When we first boated along here in 1978 you were still required to pass through a pair of fabricating sheds, as though through the middle of a factory floor. Workmen looked up from their machines and mouthed inaudible greetings, though they may have been imprecations. You waved at shunting engine drivers, you saw crocodiles of steelworkers shuffling across the canal at the end of their shift, you saw cranes, you saw forklifts, you saw … *industry*.

Rob found difficulty in grasping the concept of 'industry'. He had grown up in a world where people had stopped making things as a means of earning a living, and gone over to haranguing for the most part innocent strangers on the telephone instead. At Middleport we encountered a couple of potteries still going defiantly about their business,

– nicknamed 'The Knobsticks' – had carried china clay down from the Mersey ports to the pot banks of the Six Towns for the best part of two hundred years. In those days the canal played as significant a role in the comings and goings and imports and exports of North Staffordshire as the A500 trunk road does now. Next door, the Newport Pottery – famed for its connections with Clarice Cliff – had been demolished and replaced by modern flats. I remain to be convinced that this shotgun wedding between housing and canals is good for either party: the occupants expect more from their view than Canada goose droppings; the boaters expect more from their journey than bras dangling from balconies.

Once they had gained a toehold on wastegrounds, saplings were maturing into trees and hiding all

trace of former factories. Imaginatively, if somewhat erroneously, conferred its title by Josiah Wedgwood, Etruria had almost returned full circle to its pastoral origins before the master potter started the whole shooting match in 1769.

At Etruria Junction we bore left at the point where the Caldon Canal commences its hike in the direction of the Staffordshire Moorlands and the Churnet Valley. We were not taken in by the milepost's promise of a thirty mile trip to Uttoxeter, a voyage impossible since 1849. I would have relished visiting Etruria Industrial Museum but it didn't open until the afternoon. Rob admired Brindley's statue and the view beyond to Shelton church: 'It could be anywhere, not Stoke,' he gasped.

'Ah, but I *want* it to be Stoke,' I thought, but refrained from saying, lamenting instead that each time I come to Stoke – for want of a less embracing name – it is a little less like it used to be. I didn't want all the left-overs cared for in a museum like the incarcerated residents of a home for the elderly,

but you couldn't help wondering how many of their peers would emerge unscathed from the recession. We saw a good many abandoned factories too, and wondered what use, if any, might ever be found for them again. 'Canal Corridor Enhancement Scheme' notice boards caught our eye at regular intervals. It was difficult to tell if that was a promise or an apology.

I pointed out the terracotta gabled premises of the Anderton Boat Company whose narrow boats

Shelton wagon, Foxfield

Etruscan Bone Mill, Etruria

I wanted them out there still raging against the dying of the light, still puffing their sulphur where the land of launderies stood.

Being the senior participant, being the 'expert', I went ahead to spy out the lie of the land at Bedford Street Staircase Locks. The accomplice hadn't encountered a 'staircase' before. He looked baffled when I outlined the subtle difference in operation that multi-chambered locks demand. He continued to look baffled when I went over the subtleties for a second time; slower and louder. I didn't blame him. Lockworking is like sex. Hearing about it secondhand is no earthly use at all.

I cursed our luck, there was a boat at the bottom of the locks preparing to go in. As I had failed to impart, staircase locks were a space-saving device which resulted in time-consuming operating procedures. I'll tell you what I told Rob, maybe it'll come over better in writing. Better still, I'll quote from the relevant *Canal Companion*:

Staircase locks are locks where adjacent chambers share common gates. When working uphill the upper chamber must be full so that water can be released to fill the lower chamber. Going downhill, the lower chamber must be empty to enable water from the upper chamber to flow into it.

You think that's opaque! In their early guides, published in the 'fifties, British Waterways'

Coming down - Bedford Street Locks

description of the technique to be employed on encountering a staircase lock ran to two pages of text, including a diagram and thirty-three sequentially numbered instructions.

In the good old days it was common practise for boat captains to solve any difference of opinion concerning whose turn it was to pass through any particular lock by resorting to fisticuffs. It is one of the charming traditions of the canals which continues to this day. Of course we're a bit more stand-offish about it now, there are even attempts to be polite … through clenched teeth. But there's no gainsaying the devil that leaps on all our shoulders when we come to a lock. Neither is there any gainsaying the born leaders who cannot help asserting their authority. One was already going about his business, pointing at people, issuing instructions, establishing priorities. His was the boat preceding ours. When I idly suggested that *Deli* would be the next boat to go up after the boat waiting above had come down, he eyed me like a Field Marshal whose battle plan had been insubordinately queried by a non-commissioned officer, and gesticulated with his windlass to the lockside notice which informed interested parties that at busy times boaters should adopt a protocol of two up two down. When I pointed out that I wasn't convinced that three boats constituted *busy*, he informed me that there were more boats coming down. 'Coming down?', for all

Going up - Bedford Street Locks

we knew they may have just left Froghall. Resistance was inadvisable. I went and took some photographs. In the final analysis it took us three-quarters of an hour to negotiate that single pair of locks. Canal travel instils a heightened awareness of the futility of impatience.

One of my favourite parts of the Caldon Canal is its passage through Hanley Park. I would like to have been there in its Edwardian hey-day when the bandstand would be fulfilling its purpose and figures straight out of Arnold Bennett stories would be languorously strolling across the ornamental footbridges which span the canal. Now the terracotta-embellished pavilion is boarded up and despondency hangs in the air like a shabby net curtain.

Thank goodness then for Rob, whose raw enthusiasm revived me. Each fresh turn in the Caldon was new to him, though he was experiencing difficulty in equating it topographically with his extensive knowledge of Stoke-on-Trent as viewed by road. Such dysfunctions are a feature of canal travel. One sees familiar worlds from a fresh perspective, like seeing a new side to the character of a close friend or relation, and more often than not admiring it. Moreover, the pair of us, though ostensibly on the same journey, were each seeing things through a different filter: I had one eye cocked for the remnants of the pottery industry; Rob was looking to see where fishing might be worthwhile.

On the way through Harecastle Tunnel, he had amused me with an account of catching crayfish at the foot of Bosley Locks on the Macclesfield Canal. He had put out pots overnight, baited with lumps of gammon, and in the morning had harvested no less than eight signal crayfish, an American interloper that is slowly but surely driving the indigenous British crayfish out of house and home. 'Some of them were a foot long,' he'd recalled enthusiastically, 'I boiled them alive with garlic, they were delicious'.

We were so busy talking that we didn't see the signs labelled 'Caution - Low Headroom'. *Deli's* new chimney, purchased solely to impress visiting authors, came a cropper with an abrupt and disconcerting clang. I shuffled uncomfortably, making a mental note to underline the restricted nature of the overbridges thereabouts in the next available *Canal Companion*.

The canalscape beyond the Bridgewater Pottery had altered drastically in the couple of years which had passed since I had last researched this route. New flats had begun to colonise the waste-grounds and the towpath, formerly a cindery, puddle-laden, apology for a pathway, had been magically transformed into the sort of promenade one encounters at Spanish seaside resorts. Within no time, I imagine, pavement cafes will be springing up, obliterating the traditional street corner pubs, one of which I spotted across an as yet

Deli enters Planet Lock

un-regenerated wasteground, still proudly emblazoned above its doorway with the legend: Parkers Celebrated Ales. I was reminded of the omnipotent signal crayfish and their diminishing British counterparts.

Rather roguishly, I accepted Rob's suggestion that he go ahead to operate the infamous Ivy House Lift Bridge. Many a canalling soul has been broken on this recalcitrant piece of apparatus. The bridge carries a not unbusy road across the canal. When I first knew it, it was manually operated with a mixture of chains, barge-poles and brute force. Then some bright spark had the idea of electrifying it. All very well in theory, but could one reasonably expect the general boating public to operate a fairly complex push-button control panel without previous experience? British Waterways obviously thought so. I ventured to differ. The secret lies in the copious instructions: but, come on, let's be honest, how many of us read *them*!

Ivy House Lift Bridge

I leant on the tiller nonchalantly while Rob scurried back and forth with the air of a man bemused. He looked back enquiringly on a couple of occasions. I waved encouragingly. He was a man after my own heart. He couldn't be bothered with the minutiae of small print. But all us poets are called to account sooner or later. The organisers in life have us over a barrel. They always win in the end, because winning is what matters to them; not art. What Rob hadn't read was that you have to manually lower the barriers across either side of the bridge before the electrical components of the bridge will function. By a process of elimination the penny dropped in the end. The bridge rose majestically. I sailed serenely through.

Houdini-like, the canal began to shake off the shackles of Stoke-on-Trent and found itself traversing a shelf above the stripling Trent, not quite as romantic a location as Matthew Arnold's stripling Thames. I told Rob about the purpose-built boats which conveyed crockery for Johnson Brothers between their various plants along this section of the canal between 1966 and 1995, and how they were so speedily driven that a tsunami always followed in their wake. It seemed incredible now that they had ever existed, for the works at Milton had been reduced to rubble.

We had discussed arrangements for lunch as men of the world. After all, we were overdue another calorie intake. It was one o'clock when we reached Milton and time to adjourn. They obviously hadn't been expecting us, or any other boaters for that matter; there were no bollards or mooring rings. That wouldn't have been a problem if Rob had owned, like other boaters, a *pair* of mooring pins, but it emerged that he was temporarily challenged in the mooring pin department, having left one behind on the Shropshire Union. There was a wooden stump on the far side of the towpath which I thought might suffice, but we both realised the implications of stringing a rope across the towpath, envisaging disciplinary action together with a punitive fine. In the end Rob improvised – rather cleverly I thought – by hammering his windlass into the ground and tying the rope to that. Rather than secure the boat against the curiosity of restless natives, he remained aboard on watch, and I went in search of a fish & chip shop.

I've always had a soft spot for Milton. As the *Canal Companion* puts it, it's 'a lively little frontier post, a last chance for meaningful shopping until you reach Leek'. It helps that it has a secondhand bookshop, quaintly named Abacas, and a well-stocked one at that, no mere repository of mouldering also-rans. I was sorely tempted to dash in, and got as far as pressing my nose up against the window, but a sacrificial sense of duty, instilled by the nuns of Hinckley Convent, prevailed.

The Caldon Canal near Norton Green

The Milton Fryer is on the main road. There wasn't anyone else waiting to be served when I got there. Rob had requested sausage and chips with gravy. I plumped for fish and chips. The fish was cooked fresh for me while the conversation turned to Christmas. Obviously not a lot happens in Milton, I thought, this being August. I had timed my arrival well, within minutes the tiny premises had filled with what appeared to be a coach party. They were queueing down the street when I left.

While I had been away, Rob had watched two lads fish a bicycle out of the canal with an anchor at the end of a rope. Had they known where to look, or was this some local form of angling? We couldn't decide. I drew Rob's attention to the nearby Hardman Football Development Centre, imagining it churning out a conveyor belt of young Norman Hunters, Chopper Harris's and Billy Bremners. It is a sad reflection on the emasculation of the modern game that one has to go so far back in history to find suitable role models, Roy Keane and Patrick Vieira notwithstanding, they were far too gentlemanly.

We got away from Milton at one-thirty. Two or three bridges along, a gang of youths had accumulated in the twilight of the bridge-hole. For all we knew they may have been innocently discussing arrangements for a flower show, but their presence was intimidating. Rob reckoned they resembled monkeys, and could trace their evolutionary steps from jungle branch to canal bridge in a direct, Darwinesque line. I knew what he meant, though I knew also that an absence of trust escalates, that's why wars start. Canals, in common with football, have a history of attracting hooligans, they are both easy targets. The conjuring trick is – and I'm not claiming it's an easy one to master – to eradicate the root cause of tension at source. In other words, something so rewarding – and so tiring into the bargain – that violence and abuse never enters their darling little heads.

That latter-day Johnson and his Boswell reached Engine Lock, at 12 feet and 1 inch, one of the deepest narrowbeam chambers on the canal system. It derives its functional name from the existence of a pumping engine in the vicinity of the long vanished Cockshead Colliery. There was a boat-building yard and a dry dock here as well. Now there was just a cottage and a postman delivering a parcel. I opened the upper paddles and peered down at *Deli*, so far below that it looked like something inadvertently caught in an elephant trap. Rob was yawning. He was used to two hour stints at the tiller, not nine! The sight made one rapidly ageing man feel very happy. After all, his accomplice was a palpably super-fit young man of twenty-five, a regular bagger of Munros, who could modestly count himself amongst the top forty badminton players in the country.

Beyond Engine Lock it all began to get very pretty. The feeder came inconspicuously in from Knypersley reservoir. No bigger than a brook, the Trent got piped beneath the canal. There were two lift bridges which needed winding up hydraulically with a windlass, a far less Byzantine operation than back at Ivy House. Now there were pastures on either side, and woods with wheeling buzzards. Rob was eyeing up the hedgrows and thinking of blackberry jam. Many of the blackberry bushes were on the opposite side to the towpath, beyond the reach of mere pedestrians, exclusive bounty for boaters.

And so we came to Stockton Brook and a flight of five closely spaced locks which would carry us forty feet up into a new landscape of small holdings and drystone walls which owed something to the Pennines. To stave off lassitude, Rob offered to operate the locks. I readily agreed, it was nice to be back at the tiller again: fine-judging each unblemished entry into the lock chambers; ensuring, even against a surreptitious undertow, that the bow

and stern were not impaled on the gates; enjoying the sensation of rising from the dripping, diesel perfumed depths to a fresh new vista. Halfway up, I caught Rob sprawled out on a lock beam, resting from his labours. Erstwhile conqueror of Tardebigge, Hatton and Devizes, I knew the feeling, he'd survive.

After the locks Rob went below to brew some tea. The canal continued in a north-easterly direction, traversing its summit section, reed-lined, and with a very real sense that it was heading for the hills. Rob emerged from the hatch with the teas, looked about him, and shook his head.

'It looks like a river. I'm not sure I'd like to take *Deli* on a river.'

'You will,' I sought to reassure him. 'You just need a bit more experience. Boating on rivers is fun. You ought to go down the Staffs & Worcs and try the Severn sometime.'

'The Severn! It floods doesn't it?'

'Yes. But they don't allow you to boat on it when the current's too strong. We were once the last boat allowed onto the river at Stourport before they closed it to navigation on account of heavy rainfall. We went down to Worcester in record time and had to start turning by the cathedral to ensure we were facing the right way to get into Diglis Locks, a quarter of a mile downstream. If we'd left it any later we'd have ended up going all the way down to Gloucester, sideways.'

Stockton Brook Top Lock

cooling off period

On reflection, this probably wasn't the best tale to encourage Rob to attempt river cruising, I expect – rather like our boat that day on the Severn – I just got carried away.

Seeking to change the subject I asked about the solar panel on *Deli's* cabin roof.

'Yeah,' said Rob with a casual air. 'That makes me all the electricity I need. It stores up in the battery. I got a wind turbine too, but I bought the wrong sort of pole to fit it on. But now I don't think I need it anyway. I don't have a television, just a cassette-player.'

'What kind of music do you like?'

'Classic stuff, really,' Rob said, after a moment's thought. 'Dire Straits, Clannad. At the moment I've only got one cassette … well, actually it's a set of three, a compilation of disco hits, only when I got it back to the boat I found there was one missing. I bought it at a charity shop too. Imagine being *done* by a charity shop,' he added ruefully.

I was beginning to warm to Rob's happy-go-lucky lifestyle. He wasn't exactly New Age – and you do see plenty of them on the canals – but he was certainly outside the system, and I don't mean *canal* system. When we reached Endon he began looking about him more intently. Part of his thinking in kindly making the boat available for my trip was an idea germinating in his mind to winter on the Caldon. He had been toying with the idea of 'going back to Uni', taking up where he'd left off doing a

Sports Science degree. He reckoned it would be 'dead easy' to commute down the towpath to Stoke on his bike.

We 'arced round Endon' – as the *Canal Companion* poetically puts it – noting the services block at Park Lane Wharf where Rob, should he decide to stay, would have access to shower, toilet, laundry, and rubbish disposal facilities; all the benefits of civilisation in fact. Besides, he had friends in Endon, 'on Station Road'. After Park Lane I clicked (with embarrassing ease) into guide book compiler mode and launched into a lecture concerning the original layout of the canal.

'When the Caldon was first built in 1779 the summit ended here at Park Lane and proceeded at a lower level, pretty much where the old railway is down there, do you see?'

Rob nodded, politely, if not exactly encouragingly. I continued: 'Then when they built Rudyard reservoir and the Leek Branch, they had to bring that in at the summit for the sake of the water supplies, so they extended the summit from Park Lane to Hazelhurst, which is the bit we're going along now. When they got to Hazelhurst they built a staircase lock to take the main line down towards Froghall only, as we saw back at Etruria, staircases are time-consuming and they also tend to waste more water.'

Rob's expression had become somewhat glazed, but I had started and was determined to finish.

'So in 1841 they hit on the present arrangement whereby the Froghall route drops down from Hazelhurst Junction through three separate locks before passing beneath the Leek Arm which is carried across it on an aqueduct. It's very interesting really,' I added lamely.

A silent interlude ensued, during which we both grappled with our own thoughts. Almost subconsciously I noted some meadowsweet growing on the canal bank, and got to thinking that it hadn't been a prolific year for meadowsweet. Then I began recalling some of my previous visits this way, and how, when we'd first cruised the Caldon in 1978, the railway was still busy with goods trains carrying sand from Oakamoor and stone from Cauldon Low. I suppose if I was pressed to name a favourite spot on the whole canal network, Hazelhurst Junction would be up there challenging for that accolade. Back in 1978 we coveted the junction house, notwithstanding that it appeared to lack mains water and electricity. Its location approached perfection: a canal junction on your doorstep; a working railway at the rear; proximity to the 'Queen of the Moorlands', alias Leek.

I alighted at a convenient bridge and walked ahead to take some photographs. A boat was waiting to go down through the locks, but had been held up by another boat which, in trying to essay a sharp turn to the left out of the top lock and on to the Leek arm, had got well and truly jammed. Its skipper decided to tie up while he worked out his angles for another attempt. *Deli* cruised blithely by and bore right in the direction of Leek. Despite the fact that it feeds significant volumes of water into the summit, the Leek arm itself often seems distinctly shallow and progress, consequently slow. I took a picture of *Deli* as she crossed the aqueduct over the main line. Down on the lower canal I could see the Hollybush Inn, a popular pub famous once (and for all I know still) for its tug-of-war team. Another aqueduct, more modest in design, carries the arm across the old railway. I peered down over the parapet, but all I could see was a jungle, even though the rails remain in situ. A good number of boatowners choose to moor along the arm, and several of them were working on their boats; an abiding passion if you're so-minded.

What with the moored boats and the shallow channel, Rob was travelling at a snail's pace even by canal standards, where the maximum permitted speed of 4mph is something rarely achieved. I waited to be picked up at Bridge 6 where the Staffordshire Way crosses the canal.

Eventually *Deli* came chugging into view. I got back on board and watched, with Rob, a sequence

of lovely gardens gliding by. Most of them ran, in layered terraces, sublimely down to the water's edge. Soon, though, we left the houses astern, plunging into a thick belt of woodland, like something out of Hansel and Gretel. If the essence of canal travel is escape, then you could say we had successfully completed our mission. We hadn't come much above ten miles from Etruria, but you'd think we'd crossed a continent.

I wondered if escape was something which ever crossed the minds of the former inmates of St Edwards, the County Asylum, whose gloomy tower protuded above the treeline on the opposite side of the valley. The irony is that, following closure of the hospital, the grounds and some of the original buildings have been transformed into an exclusive housing development. The tower itself – a water tower originally – had been converted into an eight-floor, five bedroom family home, and was on the market for three-quarters of a million!

Opened in 1897, St Edwards was a massive undertaking, replacing a number of local asylums throughout the county. With a sports ground, hospital, church and cinema, it was a community within itself. So much coal was required to fuel its boilers that it had its own electric tramway built to bring wagons up from the Churnet Valley railway at Leekbrook.

Rob was less interested in the history of the asylum than the presence of pike in the margins of the canal. 'There's one, he's a big lad, did you see

Hazelhurst Junction

Leek Tunnel Pool

him?' he gestured, but all I saw was muddy water and the ripples of a vanished splash. I had promised Rob an exciting dénouement to the arm's passage through the upper Churnet Valley. Earlier he had enthusiastically recalled mooring overnight at Tixall where the Staffordshire & Worcestershire Canal widens elegantly into an ornamental lake. I hinted that the Leek arm could match that, and some. So when we rounded a bend and found the canal splaying out into a broad pool fringed by low hills, I watched for a genuine look of amazement to register on his face. I would be guilty of exaggeration if I told you he looked amazed, but he did say 'this is a tidy spot', which I took as high praise in North Staffordshire circles. Moreover I could see him thinking that there would be a good many fish to catch.

The only way out of the pool – unless you commit the blunder of turning back – is to enter the sandstone portal of Leek Tunnel, 130 yards long. Having hewn their way through Harecastle Hill, this toy tunnel to Leek must have seemed like child's play to the navvies. *Deli* fitted into it so snugly that we could have let go the tiller.

Now for the anti-climax! Once upon a time the canal continued to a terminal basin reasonably close to the town centre, by the old railway station in fact. Both have long since vanished, and in their place, as befits the Philistine age we live in, a supermarket stands. Goodness knows who was responsible for allowing the last half mile of the canal to be filled in. Writing at the time, in high dudgeon, the canal

stalwart, Robert Aickman, wrote despairingly that the terminus had been 'modernised into a rubbish tip', which put it rather succinctly.

Arriving by boat at the foreshortened end of the Leek Arm these days, canal travellers are faced with a bleak trudge through an industrial estate if they want to reach the town centre. It wouldn't surprise me if a high percentage of them don't bother, which is a terrible pity, because Leek is a lovely town.

The last full-size winding hole is a few hundred yards short of the end of the canal. Some of you will be wanting to know what a winding-hole is, let alone how to pronounce it! A winding-hole – there, that's three times I've written it – is a turning point, most stretches of canal lacking sufficient width for a full length traditional working narrowboat of seventy feet in length to turn around. Thus it was necessary to provide specially widened pools at strategic intervals for a boat to be turned in. In boatman's parlance these became known as winding-holes, and the important thing to remember is that the term is pronounced as in the thing which blows, and this is thought to be because a canny boatman would allow the wind to do as much of the work in turning his boat as possible.

A notice by the last winding-hole on the Leek Arm warns that boats over forty-five feet in length should proceed no further. That suggested that with *Deli* we had seven feet to play with, but of course that simple subtraction took no account of the low water levels we had been experiencing. When we reached the very end of the canal – where the narrow feeder channel slips in almost apologetically from Rudyard – it was visibly apparent that we would have our work cut out to turn the boat around.

Rob had probably spent more time on his boat in the six months he had owned it than I had spent on boats in thirty years, but one look at his worried expression told me I must pull rank and assume control. Received wisdom suggested that *Deli's* stern be kept in the deepest water, but given the configuration of the canal that was a theory impossible to adhere to. I told Rob to put the bow into the widest point as far as it would go and went forward in the hope that I could leap off the front of the boat with the bow line. Another principle, which had somehow stuck in my far from practical brain, was that the less you used the engine in such circumstances the better; the propellor having a tendency to pull down the stern. It would also be better if there was only one person left aboard. Two people would double the weight; or perhaps even triple it on this occasion!

Poised uncertainly on the gunwale (the narrow strip of hull protruding from the cabinside), I tried to judge where I might land safely, without ending ignominiously in a combination of water, mud or clump of reed. I had never shone at jumping at school, even though my teachers had often been heard to say: 'Pearson, you're in for the high jump!' But over the seemingly interminable years of my canal writing career I had somehow acquired quite an art in leaping from a standing start: to give you some sort of visual equivalent, mine is a style of action not dissimilar from that of a jump jet taking off from an aircraft carrier.

Mouthing a prayer to St Werburgh, patron saint of skydivers, I made my leap, hung in the air long enough to hum the first two verses of *Leaving on a Jet Plane*, then landed on firm ground, narrowly missing a collision with a passing dog-walker. I looked around, expecting some applause from Rob, but he was far too busy thrashing the other end of the boat around in the treacle-like margins of the opposite bank. He looked like a man rotovating a dung heap.

Signalling that he should put the engine in neutral, to reduce the undertow, I began to pull on the bow line. We could have done with that tug-of-war team from Denford, but in the end we got the bow round and found ourselves facing the way we'd come. Punching the air as if we'd combined to score the winning goal at Wembley deep into injury time, we tied *Deli* up to the two mooring rings altruistically provided by the local authority in partnership with British Waterways and an *entourage* of other stakeholders to encourage tourism in Leek. A small ceremony was called for, but the dog-walker had gone, and there was no one there to acknowledge our achievement. 'A bit different from the reception afforded that young round the world yachtsman,' I

Will it fit? - Leek Tunnel

Nicholson Memorial

thought, and yet who was to say the two feats weren't on a par? And I wouldn't mind betting, in the final analysis, that young Mike Perham would have swapped all his exotic experiences for an oatcake from Brenda's.

Stiff upper-lipped to the last, Rob and I shook hands perfunctorily. He was staying aboard to cook himself a steak – as the afternoon had worn on his calorie count had plunged to worrying levels – and I was going to brave the industrial estate in an attempt to prove that canals and Leek could co-exist given decent signage.

The shops were all shut by the time – some twenty minutes later – I reached the town centre. I didn't consider that much of a setback ... I wasn't there for the antiques – which have replaced silk as Leek's main stock in trade – I was there for the architecture. And *what* architecture! For a town of its modest size and comparative isolation, Leek punches well above its aesthetic weight. A good deal of the credit for this lies with a family firm of Victorian architects, Sugden & Son.

William Sugden (a Yorkshireman, as befits someone with that surname) had come down from Keighley in 1849 to work for the North Staffordshire Railway on the designs for some of the stations along the Churnet Valley Line. He settled in Leek and his son, Larner, was born in 1850. At the age of sixteen, Larner was apprenticed to his father's practice whose offices were in Derby Street, in a building now occupied by Boots. The Sugdens work includes the Nicholson Institute of 1884 on Stockwell Street which houses the library. I had recently dropped in to see an exhibition devoted to the life and times of Sir Thomas Wardle who, you'll remember, owned Swainsley Hall in the Manifold Valley. I have a penchant for such historical connections. Wardle was a great friend of, and collaborator with, William Morris, who frequently visited Leek in the 1870s to

work on his textile designs at Wardle's dyeworks. Morris became friendly with Larner Sugden, and it is said that, in saving the 17th Century house called Greystones from demolition during construction of the Institute, they sowed the seeds for the establishment of the Society for the Protection of Ancient Buildings.

In recent years Greystones had become a justly celebrated tea room. A while ago I was saddened to see that it had closed its doors to the public. But all, apparently, is not lost, I have it on good authority from an enthusiastic young woman in the Tourist Information Centre, that Greystones' charming owners, Janet and Roger, have reinvented themselves a few hundred yards up the road at Church Street Clocks & Time For Tea.

I have got somehow side-tracked, but, it's only fair to warn you, that is easily done in Leek. I wanted to tell you more about the Nicholson Institute, about the bas-reliefs of Shakespeare, Newton, Reynolds and Tennyson which adorn its façade, about the frescoes depicting Literature, Art and Science which you can just about see on a rear wall if you poke your head out of one of the windows in the Gentleman's Lavatory … I am in no position to confirm or deny whether the same view is available in the Ladies, nor to elaborate on my reasons for poking my head out of the lavatory window in the first place.

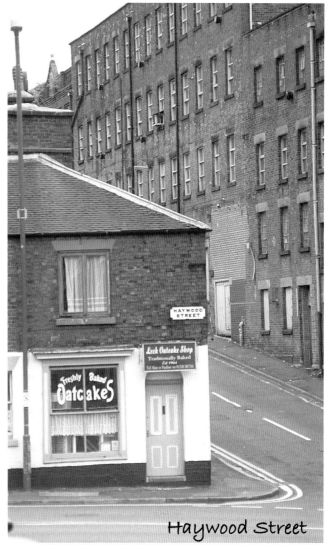

Haywood Street

75

The same Nicholson family who sponsored the Institute, also caused one of the town's other landmarks to be erected, the Nicholson War Memorial, built in 1925 in memory, specifically, of Basil Lee Nicholson who was killed at the Battle of Ypres in 1915, and of all the other four hundred and nineteen residents of the town who fell in the First World War. Some of their battlegrounds are carved beneath the memorial's four clock faces: Hooge, Loos, Ypres, Somme, Bellenglise, Ramicourt, Bohain, Lens, Gommecourt; evocative names from the killing fields of Flanders. In 1949 it was necessary to append a further one hundred and one names of men from the district who had perished in the Second World War. In 2005 fifteen additional names were added recalling victims inadvertently left off the 1949 plaque, one of which, rarely where war memorials are concerned, commemorated the only person killed in Leek during a bombing raid on the town in 1941.

The Arts & Crafts styled NatWest Bank in Derby Street is another Sugden building, as is the former Police Station on Leonard Street near the bus station: wherever they moved to afterwards, the bloodhounds of the law cannot have been so exquisitely housed. I'm a little surprised that Wetherspoons haven't

Nicholson Institute

requisitioned the building and re-opened it as a pub called The 'Ello 'Ello 'Ello. During their era, Sugdens, as you can see, were rarely upstaged, but one can't help wondering if there was a degree of professional rivalry at stake when Norman Shaw was called in to design All Saints' Church, Compton, and Spout Hall on St Edward Street.

If I had to step in and save any buildings in Leek, however, it would be the textile mills, which rear up, suddenly, all over the place like fugitives from a Lowry painting. It is these leviathans which define the town, and which lend Leek the illusion of being another Rochdale or Oldham or Burnley, albeit on a smaller scale. Quite a different sort of mill altogether is Brindley's Mill, a water-powered cornmill built by James Brindley of canal fame in 1752. Appropriately enough, the Churnet drives it and, since having been restored in 1974, it opens to the general public during the summer months on Saturday, Sunday and Bank holiday afternoons.

I could have walked round Leek all evening, but I caught the bus back to reality instead. They had the road up in Endon and it seemed to take a lifetime to get back to Hanley. I got home that night fourteen hours after leaving it, beating Mike Perham's nine and a half months by a comfortable margin.

Walking Backwards 3

THE Glacial Boulder was looking a bit sorry for itself, faintly apologetic about the plinth it lay so incongruously upon. Somewhere I'd read that the concreted foundations had been the base of a First World War water tower. The nearby trig point had more dignity, at least it didn't pretend to be what it was not. A linear declivity might have been the course of the old Tackeroo Railway, but with silver birch growing prolifically up along it, I couldn't be totally sure.

Even though it was overcast, I could see for miles. A few yards east of the Glacial Boulder the land tumbles away into the Sherbrook Valley. On the horizon, roughly north-east, I could see the Staffordshire Moorlands which gave some indication of the distance still to be walked. But I didn't want to get ahead of myself. A day's hike of nineteen miles would get me to Uttoxeter, three-fifths of the Staffordshire Way in the bag.

'Four dogs, every day of the year, chances are it'll happen sooner or later,' a woman was enigmatically saying to a man with an Irish Wolfhound as I passed. I would never know what *it* was. The broad, firm path descended into the valley through bracken and heather and tall waving grasses. I passed through a cloud of midges and came to the banks of the Sher Brook, chuckling past ferro-concrete foundations that I took to be the detritus of one war or another.

After two relatively hot and sunny days on the Staffordshire Way, it was refreshing to be cool. With the breeze behind me and the gradient in my favour I strode through the valley at a rate of knots that any ghosts of marching infantrymen present would have approved of, or at least recognised. I reached the Stepping Stones, a well-known nodal point for Cannock Chase explorers. Thereafter the path began to ascend, though nothing too onerous. A sign informed me that I was skirting Brocton Coppice, an area of ancient woodland. A cock pheasant's colourful head peeped round from behind a fallen bough and winked at me, as if sharing a joke.

Presently the drone of traffic interrupted my deciduous reveries and I reached the car park at the foot of the Satnall Hills. More litter! For half a mile or so the Staffordshire Way has no alternative but to follow the A513, about half of that distance without the benefit of a pavement. I was reminded of amusing passages in John Hillaby's seminal *Journey Through Britain* when, in walking from Land's End to John O' Groats, he occasionally had no alternative but to run the gauntlet of the motoring fraternity. His response was to conduct imaginary court cases in his head from which he would emerge a victorious and fêted champion of the downtrodden pedestrian. As if to emphasise the deadly nature of the road, I came upon one of those verge-side shrines which are increasingly a part of the British landscape. The flowers were fresh, the victim still missed.

So you can imagine my relief when the Staffordshire Way turned its back on the road and entered the grounds of Shugborough. Almost immediately I found myself crossing the West Coast Main Line railway and appreciating the stirring view granted generations of engine drivers as they entered Shugborough Tunnel. Not only were they confronted with the splendid 'Egyptian' decoration of the tunnel's eastern portal (the western is 'Norman' in style), towering in close proximity above it stands one of Shugborough's most flamboyant follies, the Triumphal Arch (modelled on the Athenian Arch of Hadrian), built between 1761 and 1765 in memory of Admiral George Anson who had circumnavigated the world aboard his ship *Centurion*. Genetically geared to champion the insignificant, however, I was equally enthralled with a close view – over the opposite parapet – of a small boxed aqueduct conveying a leat to the watermill located alongside the estate's home farm.

There was a certain elan to be savoured in marching past the ticket office and quietly observing the queue which had formed for those *paying* to get into the grounds. As a long distance traveller I was above such petty transactions, and I said as much to the longhorn bull scratching himself on a gatepost beside the millpond at the farm. 'I don't have to pay to get in either, and on top of that there's the perks

of the job,' he seemed to be saying. I drew alongside another impressive folly, the Tower of the Winds, and then caught sight of the hall's handsome east front and its tremendous eight-column portico. As I looked, a man in a linen suit and tie skipped self-importantly down the steps: patently not a fee-paying tourist.

Leaving the grounds behind me, I came to the delightful Essex Bridge, reputedly the longest packhorse bridge in England. It spans the Trent just downstream of its confluence with the Sow, and it would be difficult to imagine a more picturesque juxtaposition. One imagines Tolkien must have been familiar with the setting for he convalesced in the neighbouring village of Great Haywood after catching trench fever during the Battle of the Somme. Similarly he would have known the Trent & Mersey Canal, still busy with cargoes then. Now it is busy with holidaymakers, and they were taking turns to pass through Haywood Lock as I arrived on the scene. I got a grandstand view of their varying degrees of proficiency from my table at the Lock House café where I sipped a hot cup of morning coffee and took a look at the map.

Whoever it was that originally mapped out the Staffordshire Way, they were incapable of disguising a predilection for canals, or perhaps it was simply that Staffordshire is full of them. There is no gainsaying, however, that their towpaths provide a useful facility for walkers, even if they remain technically not public rights of way. Staffordshire's Way for the Millennium also follows the Trent & Mersey Canal between Great Haywood and Rugeley.

Trent & Mersey mileposts measured the next section of my walk. They fall into two categories: the ones that were originally cast by Rangeley & Dixon at Stone in the early 1800s; and replicas erected by the Trent & Mersey Canal Society in recent years. The first I encountered east of Great Haywood belonged to the former. It told me that I was fifty-five miles from the northern terminus of the canal at Preston Brook in Cheshire and thirty-seven miles from its eastern extremity at Shardlow near Derby. The River Trent, flowing peacefully alongside, did not have the benefit of mileage calculations.

Little Haywood merges amorphously into Colwich, but both villages are largely out of sight and mind where the canal traveller is concerned. I was tickled to see that the bridge which carries the railway over the canal above Colwich Lock is numbered 71A by British Waterways and 134 by Network Rail. I wondered if it received counselling to overcome its split-personality. The lock-keepers cottage was freshly whitewashed. A boat was passing down through the chamber apparently crewed by three male generations of the same family. They seemed to be enjoying a good bonding session.

Essex Bridge

I was denied a view of St Mary's Abbey, home to a Benedictine order of nuns. Instead my gaze rested on a Jersey cow and her calf penned in a picturesque jumble of outbuildings by a canalside farm below the lock. The next milepost I encountered was a replica, erected in the memory of one Lillian Laceby in 1982, as nice a way of being remembered that I can think of. Three boats went by in quick succession northwards. The first would have the next lock set for them, the others would be in for a lengthy wait, for it can take up to a quarter of an hour to fill and empty a lock.

At Wolseley I could have left the busy canal to its own devices for a while and visited the Wolseley Centre, headquarters of the Staffordshire Wildlife Trust, but I was acquiring a rhythmic imperative on these long walks which didn't take kindly to stopping and starting. Bishton Hall prep school could be seen through chestnut trees lining the opposite bank of the canal. I came upon a charming little footbridge over a spill weir designed to carry excess water from the canal into the Trent. The next milepost, another replica, commemorated a man called Frank Smith. Views of Cannock Chase gave way, rather less romantically, to Rugeley's power station. The railway came into view framed through the mellow archway of Bridge 69. I was enjoying this interweaving of my modes and routes and, as if on cue, one of the London Midland locals swished by.

Just short of where the canal crosses the Trent, the Staffordshire Way leaves the towpath, goes over the railway, and heads towards the village of Colton. A barrier had been erected across the lane by Lichfield District Council to 'restrict unauthorised vehicular access', and to 'minimise the dumping of hazardous waste and anti-social behaviour'. A case of the nanny state gone mad? Or can we simply not be trusted? I imagined the only section of society to be thwarted by the barrier would be harmless train spotters.

A lengthy wall separates the B5013 from what had once been the gracious parkland of Bellamour Hall, demolished before the last world war, though I thought I could detect some ruins by the farm buildings which remained. I crossed a potato field and reached Colton where I found a ford, a bridge, and a squat little church. The date on the village school was partly eroded, but I thought it read 1862. It was topped by a bell-cote and a weather vane, whilst the clock, whatever its age, was bang on time. Queen Anne and sizeable, Colton House (offering superior accommodation) returned my gaze inscrutably. I turned left along Reading Room Drive, skirted the village hall which must have taken its place, passed a children's play area, and found myself on a rudimentary football pitch with a pronounced slope from side to side. A tree planted to commemorate the 50th anniversary of Colton

Produce Group caught my eye, and then I was out into a patchwork of fields, navigating half by map, half by waymarker.

In one field the hay had been cut and whisked fragrantly up into rows to dry. In the following field the harvesters were still at work and a pair of noisy tractors roared intimidatingly up behind me. Next a field consisting almost entirely of thistles, then one resembling a lawn, and then a paddock, potentially a minefield of dung. Finally, a tiny field of lush grass sprinkled with circular bales of desiccated straw which gave every appearance of having lain there since the previous summer. No one would argue that there was not variety!

And so to Stockwell Heath where there was a pond so thick in lilies that it looked like an ornamental garden or a painting by Monet. A pair of Aylesbury ducks and a flotilla of chicks were bravely trying to force a passage through this morass of vegetation. I wished I'd had a picnic to enjoy on one of the pondside benches so thoughtfully provided. At a bifurcating of lanes, my heart sank at the prospect of a fenced off path along the margin of a field, but it proved better maintained than any of the examples of this approach I had encountered so far. So well maintained, in fact, that I only got stung once.

Pausing to look back for a moment, I realised that I had been steadily, if imperceptibly climbing out of the Trent Valley. Breasting the rise by the ruins of Medleywood Barn, I was rewarded with a glorious view of Blithfield Reservoir. This part of the Blithe Valley was dammed by the South Staffordshire Waterworks Company in 1953. The resultant reservoir spectacularly occupies almost eight hundred acres – a veritable inland sea – and, given our island race's latent maritime longings, doubles as an inland resort, hence the incomparable Ashmores (est. Uttoxeter 1932) ice cream vans invariably and strategically sited where the B5013 swoops down to cross the water on an elongated causeway. Trout fishing, sailing and bird-watching are additional pastimes. One is grateful that speed-boating and water-skiing are not. Incidentally, the reservoir was formally opened by the Queen Mother who had arrived (amid much fanfare … military bands, soldiers and the like) by special train at Rugeley Trent Valley, being conveyed to the reservoir in a Rolls Royce. Later the same day – as if she hadn't had enough excitement – she was shown over the Lotus shoe factory in Stafford.

Perhaps the breathtaking view blinded me to the course of the path, but I couldn't find my way over a barbed wire fence in a manner which tallied with the route as depicted on the map. After quartering the ground like a retriever who had inadvertently lost track of a bird that his master had just shot from

Stockwell Heath

The Horn Dance - Abbots Bromley

the air, I gave up and gingerly clambered over the fence without incurring any rips in either my clothing or my posterior. It goes without saying that I hadn't proceeded more than two hundred yards before I came upon the elusive stile.

It would have been nice to have been able to traverse the head of the dam, but perhaps too much to expect. Instead the path lay prettily enough beside the banks of the Blithe. I toyed with the idea of taking off my socks and shoes and paddling, but I was growing hungry and thirsty and thought it better to press on to the fleshpots of Abbots Bromley.

It was nearly one o'clock when I reached there. I'd been walking for four hours. What I wanted more than anything in the world was a pork pie and providentially Wilson's the butchers had one waiting for me beneath their counter. When I sought clarification of its provenance, I was gratified to learn that 'Simon makes them himself'. I refrained from any obvious quip concerning Simon the Pieman and took myself off to devour it beneath the picturesque butter cross, an hexagonal timber structure of 17th Century origin. It was, indeed, a *good* pie; nice and peppery. Washing it down with a pint of milk, I was on the cusp of gastronomic nirvana.

Abbots Bromley is famous for its annual Horn Dance which takes place, according to tradition, on 'the Monday following the first Sunday following the fourth of September', which is almost Easter-like in its complexity as moveable feasts go. Always assuming they've calculated the date correctly, folk with enthusiasm for such eccentricities come from far and wide to witness a dozen male dancers perform their ancient routine at locations throughout the parish from dawn to dusk. Half the participants carry antlers which, all the rest of the year, hang conspicuously in the Hurst Chapel behind the organ in St Nicholas's church.

An eclectic *mélange* of good looking buildings front onto Bagot Street and High Street, the principal thoroughfare. Not for the first time I was drawn to the conclusion that if Abbots Bromley was in, say, Sussex, rather than Staffordshire, its charms would have a much higher profile. One of the most successful and prestigious boarding schools for girls in Britain occupies much of the eastern end of the village and, during term time, the regular to-ing and fro-ing of well brought up young womenfolk introduces a certain *frisson* to the proceedings.

Abbot's Bromley Butter Cross

Blithfield Reservoir

Abbot's Bromley RC Chapel

Being the summer holidays such excitements were absent as I made my departure up Schoolhouse Lane; the school in question being the humble village school, not its illustrious neighbour. It was a charming backwater which terminated incongruously in a street of council built houses, most of which are probably privately owned now. Then, even more of a surprise … a delightful cricket ground. I liked the way each corner appeared to have a trick up its sleeve.

Behind the last council house, a field filled with heifers, significantly the first stock I had seen since the bull at Shugborough; and bear in mind that he was by way of being an exhibit in a museum. The landscape became more undulating. Looking back in a south-westerly direction I could clearly make out the trio of cathedral spires – the Ladies of the Vale – at Lichfield. Beyond Radmore Fields I came to a rutted lane of the sort I used to run along in childhood, gleefully imagining they were railway tracks. There were some sheep in an adjacent field. I had almost forgotten what sheep looked like.

The fields grew in size and were filled with wheat. I might have predicted an industrial approach to crop growing, but miraculously, where the path cut diagonally across one of these seas of corn, an opening of Moses-like dimensions had been left unsown. Moreover there were generous margins around the field perimeters. I offered silent but appreciative thanks to the altruistic landowner. Reference to the guide revealed that I was traversing Bagot's Park, one of Needwood Forest's ancient deer parks. I was five hundred feet or so above sea level, and I sensed that I was more isolated and remote than on any occasion since leaving Kinver. The guide astutely reflected that merely three or four agricultural employees are required to farm this landscape now, whereas in the past that total would have been multiplied tenfold.

I marched on, revelling in a breezy, top of the world sense of well-being. My joy was infectious, the air was filled with butterflies, brown spotted ones that I was too ignorant to identify. Then, just when I thought that it was my destiny to bestride these Churchillian 'broad sunlit uplands' for the rest of eternity, the countryside began to slope away and, rounding the edge of a plantation, a brand new landscape lay presented for my delectation, the limestone horizons of the Staffordshire Moorlands and Derbyshire Peak.

At Marlpit House Farm the notion of animal husbandry appeared to have been abandoned entirely. An official looking piece of A4 paper was pinned to one of the extensive range of outbuildings stating that an application had been made to convert them to dwellings. Thankfully there was still fecundity on show at New Thorntree Farm where a small field contained two expectant mothers, if the width of the Friesian cows contentedly chewing the cud was anything to go by.

On reaching Hanging Wicket Farm, I folded up Explorer Sheet 244, which had been my boon companion since the far side of Penkridge, and replaced it with Sheet 259. Now I was in Scounslow Green with memories of my bicycle ride. At Knightsland Farm they had the tractor out, flailing away at thistles. I got a cheery wave before a sheepdog came down the drive and objected vociferously to the presence of a stranger. Someone out of sight whistled him back home.

An assortment of pocket-sized fields ensued, mostly rough pasture; with the emphasis on rough. It was heavy going underfoot, like wading through rice pudding. No one, it occurred to me, would walk this way for fun. It was the preserve of the dedicated, long-distance walker. Looking up, I saw the wooded, northern escarpment of Needwood Forest and, a little anti-clockwise, the disused cooling towers of what was once Willington Power Station, far down the Dove Valley. The outbuildings at Knightsfield Farm were a treasure trove of long abandoned apparatus; junk in most people's estimation, but probably pure gold to the keen collector and restorer of agricultural machinery.

A greenway called Timber Lane was too overgrown to truly be a lane anymore, and effectively slowed my approach to Uttoxeter. Field Head Farm was home to a flock of white geese. Beyond it the spire of St Mary's poked above the ridge tiles of brash new housing. These dwellings accompanied me surreally towards the centre of town. Surreally, that is, because following a sequence of hedged-in rights of way, I didn't really see much evidence of human life, but I could hear it going on in the guise of television programmes, mowing machines, and desultory conversations. An embankment overlooking a marigold-filled roundabout brought me precipitously, and quite literally, down to earth with a bump. Picking myself up with as much dignity as I could muster, I strolled nonchalantly across Bamford Bridge into Uttoxeter.

King Edward Place

Midland Railway Grain Warehouse

Rail-Rover

SOME Station Roads seem to go on for ever. Some Station Roads don't have a station at the end of them anymore. At least Burton-on-Trent only falls into the former category. Everybody knows that it was the pre-eminent brewery town, but the evidence of this great industry is ebbing away, and ebbing fast. When I first came to live in the area as a child in the early 'sixties all the iconic companies were still very much in business: Bass & Worthington; Ind Coope & Allsopp; Marston, Thompson & Evershed; Truman, Hanbury & Buxton; Everards; and most of these, as the multiple names suggest, had been formed by amalgamation down the years. The remarkable infrastructure which knitted all these breweries and maltings and bottling plants and cooperages together was a unique network of internal railways. At one time there were so many level crossings in the town that, if you counted them all, you never came to the same total twice: a maximum figure of thirty-two has been quoted.

"Caution! These gates will be opened when the bell rings," was an injunction engraved on every Burtonian's subconscious. Pedestrians came to view such frequent interruptions phlegmatically, motorists fumed impatiently, children swung on the moving gates delightedly. In the days when I used to run the length of Station Street, satchel swinging on my back, to get from the station to my father's office (having arrived back from school in Ashby on the teatime train) I used to wager with myself to complete the distance without being stopped at one of the level crossings en route. Not that I ever minded losing; watching one of the bright red saddle tanks getting to grips with the greasy rails, and drawing its short train of brewery vans across the busy street, made a virtue out of necessity, turned an hiatus into a treat. There was nowhere quite like it in the British Isles, probably not the world! And now when you walk down Station Street, it seems stripped of all its atmosphere; an India Pale Ale shadow of its past.

The monks erected their abbey on the banks of the Trent. This remains the best bit of Burton. After winter rains the washlands flood and for a day or two it looks as if the town is on the coast. I've always thought the town's planners missed a trick. They should have arranged for it to be filled with water permanently and created a massive boating lake.

The bulky Bass water tower of 1866 would have reflected most nobly in this rippling mirror. Folk would have come from far and wide.

There are good bits in and around the Market Place too. St Modwen's parish church for example, and the Market Hall itself, of 1883, with a sculpted relief depicting King John's granting of a charter in 1200. In the grounds of the war memorial there's a tablet commemorating the local VC hero L/Cpl Coltman, whose humble birthplace I just happen to live in; there's an anchor from HMS *Resolution* (how these inland towns love their anchors!); and there are students smoking and swearing in amongst all these artefacts of sacrifice as if their threat-free lives depended on it.

I walked down Station Street with one foot in the past, finding it more comforting to look up than look down. The words ORDISH & HALL evoked memories of a family run department store who 'did' our curtains for us and to where my mother would take my aunts when they descended on us for an orgy of shopping. Didn't the CORONATION BUILDING host another store called Stockbridge's? Time plays tricks on the memory, it might have been a bit further along. In any case, it now reads COR-NATION BU-LDING. Where Worthington Way now curves in, I recall a level crossing and a Shell garage where my father was in the habit of filling up prior to departing on his lengthy business trips. At the intersection with Guild Street the MUSEUM & ART GALLERY stands abandoned, sharing its fate with the neighbouring cinema, an incredible eyesore – have the local authority no jurisdiction, let alone pride? On the opposite side of the street Sainsbury's looks smug, as well it might, this is where our needs, our appetites are satisfied now.

I arrived at the gateway to Molson Coors – 'the global family brewer' – Toronto, Montreal, Denver …and then, something of an anticlimax: somewhere …'darn it' …called Burton. At the gatehouse men in high visibility vests looked like bouncers, not brewers. At least the aroma of malt still filled the air. Coors bought out that most iconic of brewing dynasties, Bass. They don't brew beer here now, they brew brands. What's more, they've even had the gall to abandon the Bass Museum, the town's last repository of heritage and tradition.

Two or three hundred yards further on, the Ind Coope brewery has been turned into flats. The premises on the corner of Mosley Street which once housed the London Midland Region railway goods department, in which dozens of busy clerks attempted to keep control of all the beer traffics, stands empty. Half the town is *empty* for goodness sake! Samuel Allsopp's New Brewery of 1860 is home to the spirit group who lack even the pride to employ capital letters: in any case it reads 'spir-- group'. Across the railway lines stands the MIDLAND RAILWAY GRAIN WAREHOUSE No.2. In the mid 'eighties it was lovingly restored for use as office space … I should know … I had an office there myself. Now it lies empty and boarded up: so much for regeneration. What am I mourning? – the loss of my youth, the decay of a well-known place? The end of

with the equally imposing Town Hall – even if it was at first going to be used as an institute, and later the Liberal Club. According to a handily-placed interpretive board, King Edward VII – a regular visitor to Lord Burton's Rangemore Hall – unveiled the impressive statue of Michael Arthur Bass in 1911 to the excitement of a huge crowd, some of whom got a privileged view by sitting on the top deck of the town's tram cars. A remarkable monarch in many respects, but capable of resurrection, I doubted that, he died in 1910!

Down the years the Town Hall has hosted many concerts, though perhaps none more remarkable than the Chopin recital scheduled for the 6th December 1926 by the renowned Ukrainian pianist, Leff Pouishnoff. At the appointed hour he sheepishly mounted the stage and announced that there would be no recital because his Bluthner grand piano had become lost in dense fog between Birmingham and Burton.

'A Gateway to the National Forest' says the sign above your head as you enter Burton station now. Down the steps – the very same steps that I used to take three at a time all those years ago – it looks as if Network Rail are doing their bit by growing a coppice on the platform.

civilisation as we know it?

Which brought me in a melancholy frame of mind to the station. But before I caught the first train of my circular railway tour of Staffordshire, I continued over the station bridge, down Borough Road and into King Edward Place, a little pocket of calm at the north-western edge of the town where the Bass family had aspirations of making a city. They kicked off with St Paul's church in 1874, and followed this up

The ten years old version of me who travelled to Ashby-de-la-Zouch six days a week to attend school was trying to pinpoint where everything was. The station of 1883 (which even as learned an observer as Sir John Betjeman had much admired …) was demolished in 1970, taking with it the bookstall, and the buffet, and the bay platforms where trains that no longer run to places like Leicester, Lichfield, Walsall, Wolverhampton and (as we shall ultimately discover) Tutbury awaited main line connections.

'Come on Pearson!' protested my inner self. 'Pull yourself together. This journey is not going to be about what's been lost, it's going to be about what can be found. Count yourself lucky that Beeching and Marples left enough lines in the county to more or less get round it by rail.'

'Oh I do, I do,' I said, trying to avoid being sad that a road-based distribution depot now occupies the site of what was once Burton's sooty engine sheds; 17B to aficionados.

The train I had caught was going all the way to Plymouth: Tamworth seemed like short change. We sailed smoothly through the wide valley of the Trent at over a hundred miles an hour. A skein of Canada geese took off from a field of stubble but they didn't have a hope of outpacing us. The Needwood escarpment lay recumbent on the horizon. Given the speed we were going the National Memorial Arboretum almost failed to register, but for a glint of gold from the top of the Armed Forces Memorial column. At Elford a train of tanker wagons was looped so that we might overtake. Gazing further into the hazy distance, I realised that I was looking over the county boundary at Warwickshire. As we pulled into the upper level platforms at Tamworth, a London bound express hurtled through below. Years ago, before the bulk of it began to go by road and air, postal trains would exchange vast quantities of mail sacks at Tamworth on a nightly basis.

When I was young and lived in Hinckley, Leicestershire, an occasional treat involved driving along the Watling Street to Tamworth in order to visit the open air swimming pool there. If my childhood memories are not distorted, the drive was the easy part, but getting into the pool invariably involved queueing. Approaching by train, fifty years later, I wasn't even sure if Tamworth had a lido anymore, but I did know that it had once been the capital of the Kingdom of Mercia; that it had given its name to a breed of pig; that it used to churn out Reliant Robins; and that it has a SnowDome! It has a Tourist Information Centre too, quite a

good example of the breed, and I left clutching a handful of leaflets, foremostly a copy of the town's Heritage Trail. Short of an open top bus tour (and no commercial case has been made – to the best of my knowledge – for one to operate in Tamworth as yet) self-guided walking leaflets are a good way to effect an introduction to a town. The one in my hand had twenty-seven points of interest to contend with. I was interested to see how many I could assimilate before tedium or hunger or, more particularly, thirst set in.

The route lay down Market Street and on to Holloway upon which stood Bank House, a savings bank founded by Sir Robert Peel at a time when other, more well-established banking institutions were proving somewhat unreliable, all of which sounded depressingly topical. It was a handsome, Tudor-Gothic building, and I would have taken a photograph had a large bright red van not been parked in front of it.

The leaflet next drew my attention to the Brewery House which had begun life in the 18th Century as a workhouse, but had later been assimilated into Morgan's Castle Brewery, itself demolished to make way for blocks of tower flats of which the *Shell Guide* bitterly enquired 'who ever inflicted these on poor Tamworth?'

Holloway sloped down to Ladybridge, spanning the River Tame immediately below its confluence with the River Anker. Downstream, the Tame bifurcates into two channels, one foaming over a weir, and in the thus islanded meadowlands a pillbox harks back to the uncertainties and insecurities of the Second World War but doesn't merit a mention in the Heritage Trail leaflet.

I passed through the archway of Holloway Lodge and encountered the Aethelfleda (or Ethelfleda) Monument. A doughty lady, much given to repelling Danes, she was the daughter of Alfred the Great, and she governed the Kingdom of Mercia early in the 10th Century. Sword in hand, and rather Joan of Arc-like, she surmounts a column erected by history conscious locals the little matter of a millennium after her rule. Her sword-free arm avuncularly surrounds the shoulders of her young nephew, Athelstan, who subsequently became the King of England. Nearby (though again overlooked by the compilers of the leaflet) stands a Russian anchor, a trophy from the Crimean War brought back for the perusal of his home town by William Peel, one of Sir Robert's sons, who later displayed such gallantry that he was awarded the Victoria Cross.

Tamworth is fortunate to have its castle grounds and gardens, they are beautifully tended, and such

Sir Robert Peel and the Town Hall

George Street, where the leaflet rather half-heartedly tried to draw my attention to various banks and building societies.

I was much more taken with the premises of the Tamworth Industrial Co-operative Society on Colehill, opened to celebrate Victoria's Diamond Jubilee in 1897. Should you follow in my footsteps take particular note of its exquisitely decorated tiles and the faux bell-cote which surmounts its roof. In Lower Gungate I was directed to Thomas Guy's almshouses. Guy was the son of a Thames lighterman but his mother was a Tamworth woman. Following his father's death, she brought her family back to the town and Thomas was educated at the Grammar School. On leaving school he returned to London and amassed a fortune selling bibles and speculating in the South Sea Company before the 'bubble' so infamously burst. He represented Tamworth in parliament between 1695 and 1707, but subsequently lost his seat. Angrily he threatened to pull his Town Hall down and banned the town's inhabitants from occupying his almshouses, a restriction which applies to this day, so be careful who you vote for in the next election!

Little Church Lane is a quaint alleyway of cafés and restaurants. It leads into St Editha's churchyard.

'Looking better now,' announced an elderly man

are their proximity to the town's main thoroughfares, that it is easy simply to wander into them with your shopping or your sandwiches for a quiet moment in the middle of the day. With time at your disposal you might want to part with five pounds to see inside the castle, but I had been round it before – in candlelight – and didn't feel a pressing need to repeat the experience, however satisfying.

The trail led past a prominent bandstand and elaborate flower beds and across a timber footbridge into Market Street where I was immediately confronted by Tamworth's most delightful building, the Town Hall of 1701, erected at the behest of Sir Thomas Guy (he of Guy's Hospital renown) of which more will follow. It deserves a better, wider setting to do it justice, to display its full charm. In the past it has been used as a butter market and as a place to store the town's fire appliance. Sir Robert Peel delivered his famous Tamworth Manifesto speech from one of its windows in 1834 and Charles Dickens gave a public reading of his works within its handsome, Tuscan column supported walls. I considered giving an impromptu public reading of my own works for the benefit of passers-by, but the adjacent statue of Sir Robert peered so disdainfully down on me that I lost my nerve and fled down

St Editha's and the Grazier Memorial

to an equally elderly woman walking along with her shopping bags ahead of me.

'Yes, brightening up,' she replied.

'No, I mean the churchyard,' the man explained, continuing: 'I had twenty-five years here, mowing for the council.'

St Editha's is an imposing collegiate church with a massive tower, notable for its unique double-helix spiral staircase. I would have liked to have ascended it, but was given to understand that it only opens to the public occasionally. Across the square from the church, a memorial commemorates Colin Grazier, a native of Tamworth who selflessly lost his life in retrieving an Engima code breaking machine from a sinking German submarine in 1942. His sacrifice, and the subsequent decoding of the Enigma machine at Bletchley Park, is said to have shortened the war by up to two years.

Next stop the Assembly Rooms, erected by public subscription in 1899. The leaflet informed me that The Beatles had performed here in 1963. Their contemporaries, Marty Wilde and The Searchers, had gone the distance, and were being advertised as appearing soon. My Pinteresque friends from the churchyard, I felt, would be more at home at the Tea Dances held on Friday afternoons. The Assembly Rooms represented item No. 22 on the trail, and I have to confess that at this point I ran out of steam, being drawn away not so much by the prospect of refreshment, as by the promise of the local studies section of the adjoining library, where I learnt to my disappointment that the lido had long ago been replaced by a leisure centre.

Back at the station I eavesdropped on two middle-aged trainspotters bemoaning the inadequacies of politicians where railway development was concerned. 'Look what a chance they missed with the Great Central,' protested one. I wondered if they had been amongst the 'Tamworth Boys' who used to congregate in such numbers in fields beside the intersection of the two busy main lines that the Police were often called out to assert a measure of control.

Up until a year or two ago, local services along the Trent Valley section of the West Coast Main Line were provided, sporadically, by buses. Now, following completion of the quadrupling scheme, London Midland provide an excellent hourly service, ideal for the would-be train-hopper. The comfortable four-coach electric train glided smoothly out of Tamworth station and rapidly picked up speed. As a literary companion for the next few stages of my journey I had brought a copy of *The Track of the Irish Mail* with me, a nineteen-thirties guide book published by the LMS Railway for the elucidation and entertainment of its passengers. It advised me that we would soon be crossing the 'marshy margin' and accompanying 'osier beds' of the Tame and that I should look to my left to see Hopwas Hays with its 'pretty woods and larch spinneys'. Alas, the water troughs at Hademore, from which contemporary steam locomotives picked up fresh water supplies for their tenders whilst remaining on the move, were a thing of the past. But the canal remained a close companion, busier now with pleasure boats, than it had probably been in the 'thirties with boats carrying coal.

At Lichfield Trent Valley one is either faced with a twenty minute walk into the city centre, or one can hang about for a connecting train from the upper level platform to City Station; they operate half hourly. Given that I was going to be spending a good deal of time ensconced aboard trains, I elected to stretch my legs, and in doing so was rewarded with a fine view from the top of Church Street, which is named after St Michael's, not the Cathedral. On the way in I had passed the Samuel Johnson Hospital, which sort of gave me a hint about how to make the best of my visit.

Writer, lexicographer, critic – Samuel Johnson (1709-1784) was many things, but it is perhaps for his wit that he is best remembered. The house he was born in still overlooks the market place and has become a museum, visited by Johnson enthusiasts from all over the world. Appropriately enough it is also a secondhand bookshop. Appropriate, that is, because Samuel's father was a bookseller operating out of these self-same premises.

'Have you come far?' asked the man in charge in a friendly manner, stretching up from the task of arranging books on a low shelf.

Not wanting to dampen his enthusiasm, I would have liked to have answered with the name of some far flung and exotic place of origin. I think both of us were disappointed when I heard myself admit: 'Burton-on-Trent.'

The great 18th Century wit might have said something caustic along the lines of: 'Well somebody has to!' But my host had better manners, and – the smile not leaving his face – contented himself with offering me a leaflet and informing me that entry was free but that donations were quietly encouraged. With this in mind, and with just three pounds and twenty-eight pence at my disposal, I made a mental note not to outstay my welcome. He pointed me towards the stairs and suggested that I might like to begin with the audio-visual presentation on the first floor. I took his advice.

It does me no credit to confess that I cannot remember where or when I first became aware of Dr Johnson. I could swear he was not on the curriculum at school. But then neither were a good many significant figures in history who should have been, as opposed to a good many who – in my opinion – were, but shouldn't have been. It would be tedious to name names at this juncture. So it was with no little interest that I sat, in splendid isolation, to absorb the salient features of his life.

The film lasted about ten minutes and was a model of its kind, the conceit being that it was narrated by his great friend and biographer, James Boswell. Having absorbed what I could – concentration never having been a particular strength of mine – I commenced my tour from room to room. And I must tell you it was fascinating stuff. 'I was born almost dead,' was Johnson's own way of describing his arrival on earth. Bearing in mind that his mother, Sarah, was forty at the time, and that the science of obstetrics must have been suffering its own birth pangs at the time, the difficulty of his entry into the world is not surprising. Furthermore it shadowed his existence, his scarred physical appearance and his ungainly mannerisms. Throughout his life he suffered from nervous tics and strange compulsions that might be termed Tourette's Syndrome now.

For a good proportion of his life poverty stalked him too.

'I was miserably poor and thought I would fight my way by my literature and my wit,' he once recalled. With three pounds and twenty-eight pence in my pocket I was able to empathise.

Bookselling hadn't made a rich man of his father, either, and Samuel had to come back from Pembroke College, Oxford with his tail between his legs after only a year because he lacked the funds to carry on. For a while he sought to earn a living teaching ('with the strongest aversion') at a grammar school in Market Bosworth, Leicestershire. Then he dabbled in

Samuel Johnson: spruced up for his tricentenary

journalism in Birmingham, until, by all accounts, marriage saved him. An unlikely union with a reasonably comfortably off widow twenty years his senior. Though, in his own words: 'Sir, it was a love marriage, on both sides'. They were married in Derby in 1735. His wife's name was Elizabeth though he endearingly knew her as 'Tetty'. Notwithstanding his experiences at Market Bosworth, the newly married couple went about opening a school at Edial near Burntwood. It was not a signal success, in fact it only attracted three pupils, though one of them happened to be called David Garrick.

When the school folded, taking much of Elizabeth's capital with it, Johnson and Garrick set out to walk to London, in the hope of prospering as a writer and an actor in the capital respectively. Two hundred and seventy two years later, as part of Johnson's Tercentenary celebrations, two suitably frock-coated and breeched (at least for photo-shoots) Johnson scholars re-enacted this journey on foot, sensibly, if anachronistically, following traffic-free canal towpaths instead of the Watling Street route favoured by their illustrious predecessors.

London's streets were not paved proverbially with gold where Johnson was concerned. Freelance journalism was no sinecure then either, occasional work for *The Gentleman's Magazine* in Clerkenwell notwithstanding. Indeed it was not until he embarked upon the compilation of his *Dictionary of the English Language* – published after nine years toil in 1755 – that he can be said to have 'arrived' as a writer. In the wake of its success he was awarded an annual pension of three hundred pounds by George II. (Memo to Queen Elizabeth II – Your Majesty, I am still awaiting mine!)

In 1763 Samuel Johnson was introduced to a young Scotsman called James Boswell in a bookshop. The pair of them occupy respective plinths in

Lichfield market place to this day. In 1773 they journeyed to the Western Isles together and wrote contrasting accounts of their travels that remain in print to this day. I was pleased to learn that Johnson had brought Boswell back to Lichfield so that he might experience 'genuine civilised life'.

Having explored the uppermost floors of the house, I discovered that there was a basement as well, featuring a period setting of a kitchen. The museum was filling up and a certain amount of shunting had to be performed, as politely as possible, with other visitors. To avoid being crushed to death, I returned upstairs to the ground floor, where I lashed out on a postcard of Sir Joshua Reynold's portait of Samuel Johnson, together with one of the late J. L. Carr's admirable 'pocket books', ironically entitled *The Sayings of Chairman Johnson*, which cost me just fifty pence and a pound respectively.

'Enjoy that?', asked my new acquaintance, still busying himself with the bookshelves. Hadn't I just read Dr Johnson's advice that new acquaintances be made as one advanced through life, and that one should keep existing friendships 'in constant repair'? With this in mind I replied enthusiastically and positively and thrust a further pound into the donations box, leading the mathematicians amongst my readers to the inescapable conclusion that I had just seventy-eight pence left in my possession.

I caught the train back from Lichfield City to Trent Valley; I was the only person on it. My connection dovetailed neatly, and I was soon being whisked from the low level platform. As the train gathered speed I glimpsed a couple of track-workers who were manhandling a wheelbarrow awkwardly across the rails, as if nothing had changed since the days of the navvies, except for their day-glo attire.

The line traversed undemonstrative countryside in which just the faintest suggestion of Cannock

James Boswell

Chase was beginning to rear up to the west. At the suggestion of the anachronistic guide book I kept my eyes peeled for the toilet factory at Armitage and was not disappointed, great piles of shrink-wrapped lavatory units illustrating graphically that this was one aspect of life which progress has as yet not eradicated.

As far as I know (and I know a good deal!) the Rugeley to Walsall railway hasn't featured hitherto in any guide books devoted to the Great Scenic Railways of Britain. And yet it begins promisingly enough, climbing up through ripening cornfields hemmed in by forestry, its little diesel trains thrumming satisfyingly as they get stuck into the gradient, and cheerfully blowing their horns at foot crossings. There was a time when Walsall would have been part of my itinerary. Then meddlesome politicians came along in the 'seventies and created a crushingly dull sounding county called West Midlands, severing Staffordshire from its traditional Black Country enclave.

So Cannock, as far as this book is concerned, marks the end of the line, though the trains themselves carry on to Birmingham. Quite a crowd boarded at Rugeley Town, making nonsense of Dr Beeching's decision to close the line at the beginning of 1965. Thirty-three years elapsed before the Chase Line, as it is now inevitably branded, was fully re-opened, in painfully slow stages back, to Rugeley.

We pulled away past a dainty little timber signal box called Brereton Sidings – though there are no sidings to be seen now, let alone wagons being shunted – and progressed through brackeny cuttings, with here and there a rocky sandstone outcrop, into woodland glades of silver birch and Scots pine. Goodness, it might have been the West Highland – next stop Crianlarich!

There was so much to see: a ragworty field of suckling sows; fishermen as static and bizarrely

dressed as gnomes in the reedy margins of a pond; a cabbage white butterfly on a thistle; a terrace of artisans' houses whose lengthy gardens, bountiful with vegetables and washing lines, ran down to the railway fence. I could have done with this for a good deal longer, but then Hednesford announced itself, rudely awakening me in a rash of redbrick houses. Two iconic images remained with me: Hednesford No.1 signal box, and Hednesford Ex-Serviceman's Club – there is magic in the mundane, trust me.

Beyond Hednesford the landscape bottomed out. Where my old map showed a honeycomb of canals and collieries, now there were houses, on either side of the line, as far as the eye could see. Not for the first or last time, I wondered what their occupants all did for a living.

At Cannock station there were no signs for the town centre, so I followed my nose; or rather, I followed a couple of youths who didn't look as though they were going for a hike across The Chase. Hill Brow Villas (1909) were succeeded by Morrisons, a night club called Silks, a ring road and a chiropodist. What more could civilisation offer? A cash machine in the wall of the Yorkshire Bank appeared to have been provided for a race of giants. Desperate for money, I had to stand on tiptoes to use it.

Bracing myself for the worst, I found Cannock coming out to greet me, disarmingly, like the host of a party you hadn't intended to go to. Here was St Luke's, the parish church, islanded by swards of grass. Here was a plaque, commemorating those of the Ancient Order of Foresters who had 'nobly laid down their lives in the Great War'. Here was the market place, pedestrianised with a clock commemorating Henry Benton, and a bandstand erected by public subscription to mark the coronation of Edward VII. Then I was in High Green and old boys were playing bowls (as their antecedents had

being doing since 1753) and I was coming upon the Conduit Head, an hexagonal pump house harking back to the days when Cannock's water briefly rivaled Malvern's.

Somehow or other, and against my better judgement, I found myself being sucked into the shopping precinct and, against my better judgement, being won over. It was brighter, airier and more cheerful than many of these places, and it was teeming with shoppers in the bright morning sunshine. The only still patch of ground was where the man from the Salvation Army stood, holding up *The War Cry* for sale in vain. A prophet withour honour in his own little corner of Staffordshire, his kinsfolk steered politely past him, wary of catching his solemn eye.

I glanced inside the market hall, but it somehow lacked the atmosphere of its Victorian predecessors that I'd encountered elsewhere on my travels through the county. Beyond the big pants stall I caught a glimpse of a stall devoted to the making of wills. A moustached man of Dickensian demeanour sat wearily behind the counter, Cannock folk being assured of their own immortality, business was slow.

George & Berties Café caught my eye. Once there were branches of this unique institution in a number of neighbouring towns, but as I ordered my coffee and sausage sandwich I was told that this is the only one remaining. What I always liked about them was the arrangement of a central counter round which patrons would perch on high stools whilst the staff scurried in and out of the kitchen. It was theatre in the round and you had a role to play, like it or not. Sometimes you were merely an extra, sometimes you had a speaking part, and it was a question of cheerfully ad-libbing your lines.

Retracing my steps to the station, I reflected upon how nice Cannock had been, and what a pleasurable place to visit. 'Nice'! I vaguely recall Miss Upton at

Cannock

Manor House Prep School in Ashby-de-la-Zouch insisting that 'nice' was not a suitable adjective. I must have been about ten at the time, but having obeyed her for over forty years, I now appear to have exhausted my vocabulary of alternative words for 'nice'.

A little knot of prospective passengers were gathered on the southbound platform. A pair of Asian youths were ascertaining if they were on the right platform for 'Brum'. On the northbound platform I was joined by a young mother with a pushchair who was telling her offspring that if he did not start behaving she was calling in the police.

Various kinds of pilgrims make a bee line for Hednesford, and the locals make life easier for them by leaving out one syllable altogether and calling it 'Hens-ford'. Pilgrims come to seek miracles at Our Lady of Lourdes grotto; to thrill to the excitements of hot rod, stock car and banger racing at Hednesford Hills Raceway (opened on the site of a former reservoir in 1952); to visit the fascinating Museum of Cannock Chase; or to watch 'The Pitmen' play non-league football. Stepping from the train, I remained open-minded as to which of these activities would appeal to me most. Walking down from the station, I was struck by the existence of a taxi rank, which seemed to suggest a level of commerce at odds with my preconceptions. Then I came upon my first Heritage Trail interpretive board and began to realise

that there was more to Hednesford than met the eye – considerably more!

I found myself in Market Street where a row of Victorian shops in chequered brick are further made remarkable by the existence of a decorative tiled shield at first floor level. A charming little enigma, thought somehow or other to relate to the Order of the Garter, but it pales in comparison with Anglesey Lodge on the opposite side of the square, erected by Edmund Peel in 1831. Edmund's brother was Sir Robert Peel, the Prime Minister and founder of the modern police force. A keen equestrian, Edmund occupied the lodge during the summer months and trained race horses in the neighbouring Hednesford Hills. With the coming of the railway the lodge became an hotel. Now, spick and span in cream stucco, it is used for office accommodation.

According to another interpretive board I was too late to buy a hurricane lamp from Blagg's Ironmongery or a Tutti Frutti ice cream from Tribali's Italian Café, but I could have hired a fancy dress outfit from Celebration Costumes. Judging by the attire of passers-by on the pavement, most of the natives had already got theirs.

It took me ten minutes to walk to the Museum of Cannock Chase. En route I passed a handsome War Memorial and the local park opened (according to another interpretive board) in 1931, funded by a levy of a penny per ton on coal produced by the mines in the vicinity.

The museum lies off the main road to Rugeley on the site of Valley Colliery, in latter years used to train young miners. The building itself was formerly a store for the pit ponies' food. I was greeted heartily by the lady behind the counter, perhaps this had something to do with the fact that I was apparently the first visitor of the day. Admission is free, and as a newcomer (and source of comic relief) I was handed a Guide to the Galleries leaflet.

I began on the ground floor in the Local History section, which included flora and fauna as well as social and industrial activities. Here I learned about the Hednesford Hills: that they were gifted to the local council by the Marquis of Angelsey in 1933; that hairgrass and cowberry can be found; that they play host to twelve species of mammal, six hundred invertebrates, and fifty-nine species of bird; and that a herd of Dexter cattle have lately been re-introduced in an attempt to return traditional grazing to the heathlands.

Cannock Chase might have remained an unspoilt wilderness were it not for man's propensity for digging for fuel and waging war. Both activities have left their scars. Primitive coal mining was being undertaken in the district as early as the 13th Century. At its zenith, in the Victorian era, there were thirty pits at work. The last colliery in the Cannock coalfield, Littleton – about five miles west of Hednesford – didn't close until 1993.

As for the military, it was the Chase's contradictory remoteness within easy reach of an industrialised heartland that attracted them. In 1860, I learned to my surprise, the Government had given serious consideration to moving the Woolwich Arsenal here. But it was in the two world wars that the Chase came into its own; the landscape was not dissimilar to the battlegrounds of Flanders. Vast camps for military personnel were erected, veritable townships with all the trappings thus implied: shops, banks, hospitals, chapels, cinemas. In the Second World War the RAF built a camp at Hednesford. After the war it gained a new role as a training centre for National Service recruits. And even when it officially closed, in 1956, it was used to house refugees who had fled from the Hungarian uprising. I liked the story of the long steep trek up from a wayside halt on the railway I had just journeyed along, which gained the appropriate sobriquet, 'kitbag hill'.

Upstairs I found a re-creation of a miner's cottage, a living room during the Second World War, and a mock up of the inside of a coal mine. There were audio links to local people's spoken memories. I enjoyed listening to the delightful dialect of a lady called Barbara Waterworth recalling how the war years had brought emancipation to local womenfolk, empowered by employment in the munitions industry, and how they could for the first time afford to catch Whieldon's double-decker buses to go on shopping expeditions to exotic new locales like Cannock. Trips to the cinema became more affordable too.

Hednesford

'Sometimes,' she remembered warmly, 'it seemed as if the whole of Hednesford was singing 'Sally, Sally, pride of our alley' along with Gracie Fields,' in the local flea pit.

Back outside the confines of the museum, the 21st Century world appeared rather colourless in comparison. All the advantages of prolonged peace and technical wizardry seem to have spawned a vacuum of disenchantment, as though there were some inverse law of paradox concerning the relationship between fortitude and happiness. 'They may know the wisdom of that at Our Lady of Lourdes,' I thought, and steered my footsteps in that direction.

There are close parallels in the history of the building of Hednesford's gargantuan Roman Catholic church with that at Tunstall. Both churches were erected between the wars by the sheer brute determination of their priests, and both structures appear hugely outlandish in their middle England settings. When Our Lady of Lourdes came obliquely into view I thought I'd been miraculously transplanted from a former mining town in Staffordshire to a former mining town in the Department du Nord, a Lens or a Bethune. I imagine that in France the church would have been open in the middle of the day. Here, in Hednesford, it had a push button security lock. I tried keying in some salient dates in the Roman calendar, but to no avail. If there were any members of the congregation privy to the number, either they weren't in the vicinity, or they weren't showing themselves. Having attended a school whose badge featured the keys to the Kingdom of Heaven, I wondered if these had by now been replaced by a keypad and St Peter rendered redundant as a consequence. I sought solace at the grotto, but that was padlocked too.

The train went cautiously back, down into the valley of the Trent like someone descending a slippery slope. I peered through the window in vain for any obvious remains of Tackeroo Junction. At this distance in time no one can be quite sure where the name Tackeroo derived from, but best guesses include the theory that it is a corruption of 'truckeroo', or truck, a throwback to the days when workers were paid with tokens 'on tick'. Personally I can't help thinking it sounds Antipodean and I wonder if it was inspired by ANZAC soldiers stationed in the district.

Early in the First World War, to link the big camps on Cannock Chase with the outside world, a new railway line was laid from Milford on the northern edge of the Chase near Stafford to Tackeroo on the outskirts of Hednesford. The workmen who travelled over the line nicknamed its trains the Tackeroo Express and even composed a jolly song about it.

I've written the odd jolly song or two about Cannock Chase and Rugeley myself, but this is not the place to reproduce the lyrics. I alighted at Rugeley Town with a sense of keen anticipation, for I have always had a soft spot for scurrilous little towns. Indeed, I have known Rugeley off and on since the age of ten, and for some time in the 'eighties we shopped here at least once a week, drawn as much by the unassuming friendliness of its inhabitants as anything else.

In those days Lea Hall Colliery still stood cheek by jowl with both of Rugeley's power stations, A and B. But the mine, developed at the beginning of the 'sixties expressly to serve the generating plants, was closed in 1990, and Rugeley A, five years later. With them went all their characterful infrastructure and appurtenances, and having lived for a good many years with nine steam-belching cooling towers on its doorstep, Rugeley woke up one day to find just four. And instead of getting a good proportion of its coal from under its feet, Rugeley B now gets its coal from as far afield as Australia.

Before all this, Rugeley was best known industrially for its tanneries. The last of those closed in 1958, but not before it had provided green leather for the seats in the House of Commons. Before that, it had been a centre for sheep and horse fairs, a way of life hard to imagine now. But if you asked what, historically speaking, Rugeley did best of all, you'd be duty bound to answer − a good old-fashioned murder.

Dr William Palmer (1824-1856) managed to cram a good deal of decadence and debauchery into his thirty-one years. His weakness was fillies, in both senses of the term. Death appeared to follow him around. His wife died, seemingly of cholera, soon after he had taken out an insurance policy on her. The same happened with his brother, Walter; although on the second occasion, their suspicions aroused, the insurance company refused to pay out. Doctor Palmer was habitually in debt, and it was the sudden death of a friend, John Parsons Cook, after a sizeable win on the horses, that brought about Palmer's arrest on a charge of murder.

Palmer had drawn attention to himself by attempting to bribe several participants in the coroner's inquest. But the main thrust of the prosecution's case concerned Palmer's purchase of strychnine shortly before he had invited his friend, Cook, to dinner. The bodies of his wife and brother were exhumed, but nothing was revealed to suggest foul play.

Market Place
Rugeley

Christina Collins'
gravestone

The case was heard at the Old Bailey because it was felt that an impartial jury could not be recruited locally. Palmer was poorly represented. His first counsel disappeared at the last minute to escape his own debts! At best the case against him was circumstantial, but the prosecution team were far better advocates than that belonging to the defence, and Palmer was sentenced to hang.

Thirty thousand attended the public execution at Stafford Gaol on 14th June 1856. A number of special excursion trains ran from Rugeley. Palmer lived up to his reputation as a wit by remarking as he approached the gallows and saw the trap-door: 'Are you sure it's safe?'. Palmer was buried, as common practice, within the prison walls. Cook lies in St Augustine's churchyard, not far from another possible victim of murder, Christina Collins.

In many respects the fate of Christina Collins has assumed prominence over that of Dr Palmer in recent times. Her all but forgotten story captured the public's imagination when Colin Dexter used it for one of his Inspector Morse detective novels, *The Wench is Dead*. He changed the name and geographical setting, but otherwise the tale was true in its essentials, which are this:

In 1839, Christina Collins was the thirty-seven year old wife of Robert Collins, a resident of Liverpool who had been forced to find work in London. Christina had been married before, to a travelling magician, whose glamorous assistant she'd duly become, but this has no real bearing on the subsequent events other than to underline her general attractiveness to the opposite sex.

Having found work as an ostler and rented accommodation on the Edgware Road, Robert Collins sent a guinea to his wife to allow her to make the journey south to join him. It could be that the railway, only just opened between Liverpool and London via Birmingham was too new a mode of transport to be contemplated. It could be that the price of a railway ticket was beyond her means. Stage coaches were still in operation and she could have caught one of them, but fatally she opted to make the journey by canal. Canal boats of the era were predominantly concerned with the conveyance of goods, but passengers were catered for in some instances. Christina Collins paid sixteen shillings to book her passage aboard one of Pickford's fly-boats. Rather ironically it was named the *Staffordshire Knot*.

The woman and her worldly possessions joined the boat at Preston Brook, the northern terminus of the Trent & Mersey Canal near Runcorn. The boat's crew consisted of three men and a boy. Being a fly-boat, it would travel day and night, hence the need for such a large complement. By any stretch of the imagination, it cannot have been an inviting prospect for a woman to spend the best part of a week in the close company of rough boatmen. As the journey unwound, witnesses spoke of the men's inebriated state and coarse language. At Stoke, on the second day of her journey, Cristina complained about the crew's behaviour to one of Pickford's porters. She further enquired about the possibility of continuing her journey by stage coach, but either no suitable services were available or she had perhaps insufficient funds to pay the alternative fare. To boost her morale, the porter's wife joined Christina aboard the *Staffordshire Knot* for the next few miles, but by the time she reached Stone, Christina was increasingly worried that the crew would 'meddle with her', and she reported her concerns to the canal clerk there. He rather callously suggested that were any 'meddling' to take place, she should report it when she reached London. Later that evening the boat was passed by another fly-boat travelling in the opposite direction and the *Staffordshire Knot's* captain was heard to boast about what he would like to be doing to his passenger that night.

Christina was last seen alive at midnight by the lock-keeper and his wife at Hoo Mill near Great Haywood. She was sitting and screaming on the roof of the boat, volubly refusing to go back down inside. The lock-keeper's wife asked the crew who she was, and the boat captain replied that she was a passenger and that her husband was accompanying her. The following morning Christina Collins' body was discovered floating in the canal at Brindley Bank on the outskirts of Rugeley. Later in the day the crew were arrested at Fazeley. Their stories conflicted, but they maintained that their passenger had drowned herself. Gradually they began to accuse each other of interfering with the woman, though the surgeon who carried out the post mortem concluded, in the euphemistic phraseology of the time, that 'no improper connection' had occurred. Nevertheless, the three men in the crew were charged with both rape and murder, though the cabin boy was allowed to go free.

The trial took place at Stafford, the cabin boy appearing as a witness for the Crown. During the trial it was revealed that the boat arrived at Fazeley some two hours behind schedule and that the victim's clothing was torn in several places. In the event the jury, guided by the judge, returned a verdict of not guilty in respect of the charge of rape. The charge of murder was postponed pending further investigation and the next Assizes.

At the subsequent murder trial, the judge put it to the jury that they must be fully satisfied that the accused had thrown the woman into the canal and thus been directly the cause of her death by drowning. Within three-quarters of an hour a unanimous verdict of guilty was returned. All three defendants were sentenced to hang, but as they were receiving the final sacrament from the chaplain in Stafford Gaol, one of them's sentence was reduced to transportation to Australia. The other pair were hanged publically on 11th April 1840. Curiously, the executioner's assistant was the worse for drink and a volunteer had to be sought from the prison ranks. The drop at Stafford Gaol was considered less than adequate and it was sometimes necessary for an assistant to go below the gallows and tug at the hanged person's legs to complete the job. I relate this gruesome footnote because the volunteer that day went on to make a career in executions. His name was George Smith and it was he who hanged William Palmer sixteen years later.

Christina Collins' gravestone can still be clearly read in the churchyard of St Augustine's. It says: 'In Memory of Christina Collins Wife of Robert Collins London who having been most barbarously treated was found dead in the Canal in this parish on 17th June 1839 Aged 37 years this stone is erected by some Individuals of the Parish of Rugeley in Commiseration of the End of this Unhappy Woman'. The punctuation and use of capitals is theirs, not mine. Poignantly, an artificial posy of red, white and pink roses lay at the foot of the stone on the occasion of my visit.

By the standards of the present day it could be argued that Dr Palmer and the boatmen got a raw deal. In both cases the evidence against them was circumstantial at best, but on the other hand it may well be that given their behaviour they got their just desserts. From my point of view, I was just pleased that Rugeley had had not one, but two notorious cases in its history, otherwise the town's entry in Wikipedia would read rather tamely. Incidently, my old railway guide was pleased to relate the story of the deputation despatched from Rugeley in the wake of the Palmer case to ask the Prime Minister of the time to agree to having the town's name changed. He was not of a mind to allow them to do so, unless, he had suggested wickedly, they would consider re-naming it after him. And the name of the PM of the time? Why Lord Palmerston of course!

Being nearer Trent Valley station now, than Rugeley Town, I walked, crossing the Trent & Mersey Canal and the Trent itself. On the banks of the latter someone had made themselves a marvellous garden, transforming what I suspected had once been a reedy, silted mill leat into an attractively fertile feature in its own right. None of the station buildings remain, save for the goods shed, a sizeable structure which houses a firm who manufacture plastic fittings. It was too warm to sit in the shelter which passes these days for a waiting room, and it was with some relief that I boarded the next northbound air-conditioned train.

At Colwich Junction the four tracks bifurcate at the point where the old North Staffordshire route to Stoke-on-Trent splays off the West Coast Main Line. Here, in 1986, two express trains collided. Amidst over eight hundred passengers involved there were miraculously no fatalities, but the driver of one of the trains, Eric Goode, perished and a small memorial garden beside the track has been established in his memory.

Beyond Colwich the main line crosses the river again and enters the grounds of Shugborough. Recalling how I'd crossed the railway when walking the Staffordshire Way, I tried to look out for the bridge which had carried me over the line, but it was all a bit of a blur: though I did glimpse a sign measuring the tunnel's length at 777 yards; then my eardrums all but burst!

At the far end of the tunnel there was no sign of Milford & Brocton station at all, let alone the other end of the Tackeroo Line. The Staffordshire & Worcestershire Canal came alongside with lines of moored boats, and one on the move, straightening up to face the aqueduct which carries the canal over the Sow.

Stafford is one of those comparatively rare examples of a county town that hasn't gone on to become a city, but as soon as you leave the station it sets out its stall to beguile you in the shape of Victoria Park. Opened in 1908 it has everything an old-fashioned park ought to have with the exception of a boating lake. Mind you it has a river running through it, with a comparatively recent statue of its famous son, Izaak Walton, peering intently down into the water to see if any fish are there for the taking. It has a bandstand and a bowling green, flower beds and lime trees, an aviary, a hothouse, and some charmingly thatched pavilions. In short, an altogether splendid spot to put you in the right frame of mind for getting to know Stafford or just as somewhere to while away the time between connecting trains.

Euphonious street names abound: I found my way from Tenterbanks, along Water Street, then Mill Street into the main thoroughfare, Greengate Street – no ubiquitous High Street here. The main motive behind my visit was to renew acquaintance with the Ancient High House, but I wasn't about to march boldly up to the door, I was going to gently perambulate, like a considerate lover. So I peregrinated my way through side streets: Tipping Street and Eastgate Street (where the William Salt Library contains a cornucopia of Staffordshire-related books and manuscripts far too erudite for the likes of a hack such as I) and on into the town's municipal heartland, the County Buildings in Martin Street, almost metropolitan in their opulence. The Market Square is dominated by the Shire Hall of 1798; indeed, it would stand out in far more majestic settings than this.

Then, eschewing what possible delights might be found within the Guild Hall shopping mall, I wended my way to Crabbery Street to see the building where Queen Elizabeth had taken wine on her way to Stafford Castle in 1575. I found that it had been a wine bar called Palmers, after William Palmer of Rugeley. Now it was boarded up and for sale. I wondered idly if the bar staff had been in the habit of asking customers: 'what's your poison?'.

There remained the little matter of St Mary's Church, tantalisingly tucked away in a green enclave all its own. If I hadn't had a schedule to keep, I might have ventured inside, but I could see the rear elevation of the High House peeping over a neighbouring wall. It has overlooked the town's main street for four hundred years, and I didn't like to keep it waiting any longer.

The High House was built for a wealthy cloth merchant at the end of the 16th Century. It was constructed of oak, felled in Doxey Woods, two miles to the north. The building now houses a museum run by the local council. Admittance is usually free unless there is some special event on, and you show yourself round, quite informally, selecting which room to visit next as the mood takes you.

For no discernible reason I went two floors up to start with and found myself gingerly opening the door labelled Castle Room. Inside, beyond a sequence of display cases, and in front of a leaded window, through which a soothing breeze was surreptitiously gaining entry, a lady was seated at an oblong table, painstakingly stitching away at some elaborately patterned material. She seemed so perfectly in tune with her 16th Century surroundings that for a moment I thought I was encountering a ghost. But then I discounted that, because I don't really subscribe to them. Furthermore, when I tentatively said 'hello', she tentatively said 'hello' back; only her tentativeness came from a heavy accent rather than the assumption that I was a ghost.

Aspects of Stafford
The Soup Kitchen
Izaak Waltons sculpture
The High House

I broke the ice by complimenting her on her choice of location; the breeze, the light through the window. She responded in an engagingly friendly manner, while I tried to place her accent. After a few preliminaries, I chanced the question that I always like to ask, in such a way as to not seem nosey.

'Spain,' she laughed.

'That's it,' I said with a smile. 'My daughter and her fiancé have just returned from an extended stay in Cadiz' – only I pronounced it 'Cadif', so that anyone else within earshot might have assumed I was a Welshman with a lisp.

'I am from the north,' she continued.

'I once sailed into Santander,' I said, with the swagger of a seasoned globe-trotter.

'I am from a bit to the left,' she replied. 'Asturias.'

'I'm a bit from the left myself,' I confessed.

It emerged that she'd married a man from English Electric who used to have a big engineering works in Stafford. He had brought her back to his home town – with considerable pride it was easy to imagine – in 1955. She had been very happy in Stafford.

'It was a lovely town. But now, not so lovely. Many ugly buildings. Look out there,' she pointed, to the flat, blunt roof of McDonalds. Why do they do such things?'

I was hardly in a position to answer, but I felt responsible for my nation's irresponsibility when it came to architecture.

'Where are you from?' she continued, conversationally.

'Burton-on-Trent,' I replied, embarrassingly.

'Lichfield's nice,' she responded, adroitly.

Just then, two more visitors entered the room, and our exchange of abridged life stories came to a precipitate end.

'Buenos dias', I said, turning to leave.

'Ah, no', she corrected me, kindly but firmly, 'buenas tardes … it is after noon.'

The next room I entered, the Victorian Room, really did have ghosts in it, or rather two ladies chatting vociferously about ghosts.

'Yes,' one was saying, to her obviously much impressed companion, 'Most Haunted's been here, not once, but twice. Derek Acorah's been in this very room, along with the Lady Mayoress and the CO from Beacon Camp.'

'And did they encounter any spirits?' asked her friend.

'Oh yes, I think there was definitely some activity. And I don't know about you, but I've always felt this room in particular has a real chill about it.'

It seemed particularly warm to me, but I let them chatter, walking circumspectly around them in the manner that the architectural critic and topographer, Jonathan Meades, sometimes obliquely conducts his television interviews, whilst pretending to peer at the Victorian bric-a-brac on display.

Next I found my way into the Stuart Bedroom with its four poster bed and creaky floors. I took pains to admire the needlework on the hangings and bedding, because my new Spanish friend had apparently sewn a good deal of it. A young couple followed me in.

'Ooh I couldn't sleep in here!' shrilled the girl. 'I'd be that spooked!'

Down on the first floor I found the Civil War Room. There were three men got up very convincingly in Cavalier clothing by the window. I smiled a greeting. They looked stonily back at me, as if resenting the intrusion. As well they might – they were waxworks.

Charles I spent the nights of 17th and 18th September 1642 in the High House as a guest of its tenant, Richard Sneyd. A month after raising his standard in Nottingham things were not going too well. The Royalist cause lacked support in the eastern counties, and the King was making his way westwards towards the Welsh Marches where he could count on a better hearing. It is recorded that Charles spent much of his sojourn in Stafford writing letters and talking to advisors, though he did find time to attend a service in St Mary's, and to put two shots through the tail of its weathercock in an attempt to demonstrate the prowess of a new kind of firearm. For my parting shot, I squared up to the silent Cavaliers by the window and suggested that they surrender now, because I knew for a fact that they were going to lose the Civil War.

There was just sufficient time before the train, I'm glad to say, to visit one of my favourite cafés, the Soup Kitchen, tucked quaintly away on Church Lane. I'd always wanted to go up to their rooftop patio, but had never been in Stafford in the right weather conditions. Procuring a pot of tea at the downstairs counter, I carried my own tray carefully upstairs, there being an egalitarian approach to eating and drinking in this establishment, whereby you can either employ a waitress or resort to self-service.

Space is at a premium on the roof, but only two of the tables were taken, so there was plenty of room for me. Liking my tea strong, I allowed it to mash in the pot, while I took stock of my surroundings and reflected on my whistle-stop tour of the town. There was a good deal more I could have seen and done. I would have liked to have walked along the river, maybe taken a look at the gaol – to reflect upon its architecture, not, I hasten to add out of any ghoulish nostalgia for the hangings I had lately learned about. A short ride on a No.482 bus would have taken me out to see Stafford's impressive castle. I poured a cup of tea and peered out over the rooftops, gable ends and chimney pots. A pigeon swooped by in a commotion of wings.

Stafford railway station's architecture is a bit too overtly 'sixties for many people's taste, but that hasn't stopped it being listed as being of architectural value. It used to feature proudly in one of British Railway's modernisation posters. And if it all seems a bit passé now, that is easily put down to subjectivity and the passage of time. The Crewe 'stopper' left from Platform 5. I thought I could just discern where the old Great Northern Line had once egressed and thought affectionately of Bromshall Tunnel. But before I could blink we were out in Doxey Marshes, a benign landscape of bullrushes, pools and willows; part earth, but mostly water.

We went under the M6 and came alongside the Sow. Black cattle were cooling themselves in its muddy margins, but one brave beast had plunged into the water up to his ample rump. I saw an old mill that had been converted into a pub at Great Bridgeford. Then the Sow passed under the line, but what I took for it coming back, was its tributary, the Meece, of Izaak Walton fame, and soon we were passing his cottage at Shallowford and I wished there was still a station at Norton Bridge so as to enable me to get off and walk back to that piscatorial shrine.

In fact there is still a station at Norton Bridge, complete with copious signage and every indication of being in use, save for the fact that Network Rail confiscated its footbridge some years back and now you have to go by replacement bus. A footnote in old timetables used to advertise Norton Bridge as the station for Eccleshall, quietly parenthesising the discouraging reality that it lay a three-mile walk from the station.

Echoing Colwich, Norton Bridge marked a junction between the mighty London & North Western Railway ('The Premier Line') and the more parochial North Staffordshire Railway, affectionately known as 'The Knotty' to its friends and supporters. *Malheureusement* the Knotty's crimson-lake locomotives and carriages are long gone, but the company's architectural penchant for all things Jacobean lives immortally on in a number of its stations and lineside dwellings. The railway station at Stone is a fine example of this. It has only recently welcomed back trains after an absence of five years. I would have liked to have known it when it bustled with railway officials. There's something of the *Marie Celeste* about it now in its sporadic guise as a community centre.

I said as much to the elderly nun whose case I'd carried across the footbridge. Goodness it had been heavy. Gold bullion at a guess. Perhaps it was the nun who put me in a Gallic frame of mind, for I found something vaguely French about the avenue of limes which led to Station Road, or should that read Rue de la Gare? Thence workers' terraces succeed to more substantial villas before the imposing premises of St Dominic's Convent and Priory School come into view – destination, doubtless, of my new acquaintance and her booty. The buildings date from 1852 and are the work of Joseph Hansom (yes, of Hansom cab fame!) who – in common with Pugin – carved a niche for himself in Roman Catholic architecture. Across the road, Jehovah's Witnesses conduct their rival faith in a somewhat less demonstrative manner.

I turned down Margaret Street (named in honour of Mother Margaret Hallahan who was instrumental in reviving Catholicism in the town). At the foot of the street stands the former premises of John Joule's brewery stores, dated 1881. Joule's were to Stone as Bass was to Burton, and in similar fashion had benefited first from the opening of the Trent & Mersey (or Grand Trunk) Canal, and later from the advent of the North Staffordshire Railway. In the 1950s the telephone number of their High Street headquarters was 'Stone 1'! Sadly, though, they were absorbed into the Bass Charrington conglomerate, and brewing, not surprisingly, ceased in 1974.

Newcastle Street crosses the canal and I joined the towpath, passing through a little tunnel which would once have been used by boat horses, and following the canal southwards past the other side of Joule's Stores, still emblazoned with the company name and its 'red cross' trade mark, I'm happy to say. The canal has always meant a great deal to Stone, I came alongside a series of boat-building and repair docks which continue to thrive in the leisure era. Canal Cruising, whose base is here, are one of the oldest hire firms in the business. The local foundry, Rangeley & Dixon, were responsible for casting all the mileposts that measure the Trent & Mersey Canal along its ninety-two mile course from Preston Brook to Shardlow. *Cressy*, the star of L. T. C. Rolt's famous inland waterway odyssey, *Narrow Boat*, was sadly broken up here after failing a survey in 1951. In more recent times it was from Stone that Terry and Monica Darlington set out on their narrowboat to travel to the South of France as recounted in *Narrow Dog to Carcassonne*. My side of the canal was overlooked by the town's former

Aspects of Stone
Railway Station
Christina Collins' sculpture
Joule's Ale Stores

workhouse, somewhat ironically now refurbished to provide upmarket accommodation.

Suddenly, I came upon another reference to the untimely end of Christina Collins. Rather absentmindedly, I had forgotten that it was here in Stone that her request for assistance from the canal clerk was met with what we would now call corporate indifference or a jobsworth attitude. Rather late in the day, the town has seen fit to make amends, in the shape of a little wooden statue sculpted by Simon Jones, together with a plaque commemorating her misfortune. The canal itself was quite busy, with boats waiting patiently to negotiate the locks. I peered, in what I hoped was an unostentatious manner, to see if their crews were using *Pearson's Canal Companions*! Those that were received a friendly nod, those that weren't a scowl of *Just William* proportions.

I left the canal by the Star Inn - amused by the name of an adjacent hair salon: Lock Keepers – and made my way towards the High Street, passing the Swan Inn (which serves ersatz Joule's ales) and encountering yet another inland anchor on display in a flower bed. Nearby, what was once the Falcon Hotel is now a Thai restaurant, but up above street level on its gable end you can still read the inscription: 'Bents Ales and Stone Stout', a reminder that the town once boasted two breweries.

High Street is pedestrianised and conducive to sauntering. A plethora of street cafés thrive in the absence of traffic and a good deal of gossiping seems to get done. In a town of twelve thousand souls it must be practically impossible to walk up the street without meeting someone you know. Furthermore the locals have been assiduous in erecting plaques, and the keen-eyed visitor will learn about the Duke of Cumberland, who came here to put down the Jacobite rebellion; the 18th Century watercolourist, Peter de Wint; and Henry Holland, who designed the old coaching stop called the Crown Hotel.

Halfway up it opens out into a pleasant square, where the former market hall now houses the library. Next one needs to look out for Joule's old offices, now come down with a bump and hosting a Co-op. At the top end of the street decorative railings draw your attention to the origin of the town's name, thought to derive from a cairn of stones raised on the graves of two 7th Century princes, murdered by their father, King Wulfhere of Mercia, for having the gall to convert to Christianity.

High Street expires in Granville Square, prettily shaded by an immense plane tree. The former post office has been converted into a Wetherspoons pub. Now I know that Wetherspoons aren't everybody's cup of tea (if that's not mixing metaphors!) but I rather admire them on a number of counts. I like the way they sensitively refurbish old buildings and bestow upon them appropriate names; I like the way they adorn the interior walls with titbits of local history; I like the way they don't allow piped music (having long believed that the hubbub of conversation – or even the lack of it – is the best soundtrack for a pub); I like their cheap and cheerful menus; and I like the way they always have on tap a wide selection of real ales … especially if they're local ones.

The Olde Poste proved a perfect example of Wetherspoon's approach. Purely as a matter of research I had peered through its portals, and it was in the same spirit of professional curiosity that I found myself proceeding through what must have been the counter area to the sorting office at the rear. The former – high ceilinged and round-windowed, contained an arrangement of comfortable-looking sofas; the latter, a long bar. Merely out of habit I perused the ales on sale and couldn't help noticing a particular one that I hadn't come across before. It was called Foundation Ale, and hailed from an outfit called the Lymestone Brewery.

'Can I help you, sir?' asked the woman behind the bar, and it would have been churlish of me to deny her the pleasure of dispensing a pint of beer.

'I think you probably can,' I replied, sheepishly. 'Where does Foundation come from?'

'Just up the road,' she laughed. 'Someone's opened up a micro-brewery in the old Bents place. It's up past the station. You can't miss the chimney.'

'And I don't think I should miss the opportunity of sampling their beer, either,' I capitulated. And, I must confess, it was lovely beer, simultaneously hoppy and fruity. I took it back with me to the former counter area where generations of Stone inhabitants had formed orderly queues to transact the despatch of their mail, and watched the comings and goings in Granville Square.

On the way back to the station (eschewing the invitation to learn belly-dancing at St Dominic's Parish Social Centre) I talked myself into a small detour, thinking that it might be possible to purchase a couple of bottles of Lymestone beer to take home. The lady behind the bar had been right, I couldn't miss the chimney, and although the majority of the site was taken up with unconnected light industries, it was good to come upon a working brewery in what had formerly been Bents' cask store. I learned this from the proprietor who, apart from disappointing me in that they currently weren't bottling, was otherwise friendliness personified. It transpired that Lymestone were using the original brewery well water to brew with, Stone having similar hard

Stoke Railway Station

properties to its subterranean water supplies as Burton down the Trent valley.

'If anything, Stone's water is even harder than Burton's,' he claimed.

Bents', it transpired, had fallen prey to Bass Charrington just as Joule's had done, and were just as mercilessly closed down.

'Bass were just after the pubs, really,' explained the proprietor with an ironic shrug.

'Well at least you've resurrected brewing in Stone,' I said.

'Well brewing's the easy part,' he laughed. 'It's distribution and selling that's the challenge.'

I could empathise with that, the same applies in publishing, and indeed any independent commercial activity in which something lovingly crafted has to elbow its way on to a playing field dominated by big rough boys.

Smugly pleased that I had left no stone unturned, I returned to the station and took the train to Stoke. The Trent & Mersey Canal kept me company for most of the way, and I remembered that 'The Knotty' had bought it out and maintained it as a going concern rather than run it down as was many a railway company's attitude to the older mode of transport. Otherwise it might not have been there for the pleasure boats that were gliding by against an horizon bounded by Trentham Park and its landmark mounment to the Duke of Sutherland.

Then the brakes went on as we passed Britannia Stadium, home of Stoke City Football Club. The train was too deep in its cutting to permit a glimpse of the dribbling statue of the club's most famous son, Sir Stanley Matthews.

There is some evidence that when the Six Towns finally stopped squabbling enough to form their Federation in 1910, Stoke was rewarded with the brand name because it was the main railhead and since its football team were such a self-proclaiming force in the land. Certainly the station does the notion justice. It always reminds me of Huddersfield: not that there is any similarity in style, simply that they both exude more than their fair share of northern provincial testosterone. But where Huddersfield resembles a Greek temple, Stoke likes to think of itself as an Elizabethan mansion with platforms where one might reasonably expect to find the croquet lawn. In their ambitious infancy, the North Staffordshire Railway's directors hired a London architect called Hunt to bolster their already rampant self-esteem, and no one would argue to this day (even Pevsner, who considered The Potteries as a whole, an 'urban tragedy',was impressed) that he failed to deliver.

The station is part of an holistic scheme which includes Winton Square and the North Stafford Hotel which remained in railway ownership into the early days of British Railways. Nowadays it belongs to the Britannia Hotels group who advertise it as 'a

Winton Square

classical, spacious and elegant hotel, easily accessible by road, rail and air'. But to arrive by any other means than rail would be a blunder in my opinion. Thus, after paying sufficient homage to the station itself, I crossed the square (taking care not to get run over in the process), bid a hearty 'good day' to the bronze statue of Josiah Wedgwood on its sandstone plinth, and entered the hallowed portals of the hotel with all the insouciance I could muster. After all, wasn't I three-quarters of the way around my single-handed circumnavigation of Staffordshire?

Along with breweries, river ferries and football grounds, I confess to something of an avid collector's approach to railway hotels. According to my detailed records, the North Stafford represented the twenty-fourth in which I have either stayed, lunched, dined or sought refreshment. Those ticked off to date range from the Royal Station at York to the Yarborough at Grimsby; from the Midland in Manchester to Turnberry and Gleneagles; from the Queen's, Birmingham to the Queen's, Leeds. In their Indian summer days of railway ownership they could always be relied upon, to my parents' way of thinking, for comfortable standards of appointment, more than passable cooking, and philosophic – if not always prompt – service. One might add plumbing to that list of virtues, and the North Stafford didn't let me down in that respect when, after a coke with ice and lemon in the lounge, I descended into the (no pun intended) bowels of the basement to attend to a call

of nature. Fabulously tiled and envelopingly urinalled, I found myself going into a cubicle and pulling the chain for the sheer pleasure of hearing the pipework perform in all its aural panoply.

The East Midlands Trains single car diesel which conveyed me on the next leg of my railway odyssey was a bit of a come down from the air conditioned electrics I had grown used to, but it evinced a certain charm. That it resembled a bus on flanged wheels was not surprising, seeing that it had been built by Leyland in a bus factory in Workington. Rattling over the pointwork at the station throat we veered left on to the Derby line and climbed past my old elusive friend, Fenton. Beneath the floor, the engine grumbled at the effort it was having to put in. We clattered past a signal box called Foley Crossing and paused to catch our breath at Longton.

It was an education to view the most southerly of the Six Towns from so elevated a vantage point. Since I had been here on my bus trip I'd learned that the locals were campaigning to give the lugubrious girder bridge – which slices Times Square in half – a fresh coat of paint. Network Rail's response was that safety takes precedence over aesthetics. The implication being that they couldn't afford the paint let alone the manpower to cosmetically improve the bridge's appearance. Perhaps they should take a leaf out of that equally impecunious public/private body, British Waterways, and arrange for volunteer labour to undertake the task.

Viewed from the train as it crosses the bridge, Longton's Classical Town Hall of 1863 appears all the more short-changed by its setting. Yet the curious thing is that the building post-dates the railway. Racking my brain, I couldn't think of any other municipality who had willingly erected their Town Hall in so cluttered a location.

A buzzer sounded in the driver's cab and the little diesel resumed its journey, still ascending, up past the Gladstone Pottery and the parish church of St James, and thence negotiating abundantly-vegetated cuttings before plunging into a tunnel at Meir. Blythe Bridge was the next stop. Had it been a weekend I might have alighted and walked three-quarters of a mile to where the Foxfield Railway recreates something of the atmosphere of the myriad mineral lines which once served North Staffordshire.

Beyond Blythe Bridge the railway ceased climbing and the train began to zip along merrily on a falling gradient. The River Blithe came alongside. At Cresswell its waters had once found use at a large dye works, but the site is now occupied by a collection of light industrial units. A row of railway workers' cottages marked the abandoned junction of the branch line to Cheadle, now just a scar seen across a field of maize. Isolated farms and milking herds ensued. Yet another empty pocket of Staffordshire. It looked as if Himalayan Balsam had been sewn decoratively into the banks of the Blithe. Occasional sections of jointed

track recalled the railway rhythms of childhood. I saw Church Leigh on its hillside and remembered crossing the line on my bicycle ride. Wheat fields waiting to be harvested proceeded the site of Bramshall Junction and the wooded course of the old Great Northern line whose nearby tunnel mouth I'd explored.

'That's where they used to keep the diggers,' a man was explaining to a small boy at the door as the train slowed down for Uttoxeter. He was recalling, of course, the JCB works, formerly Bamford & Sons' Leighton Ironworks which had, in its hey-day, extended to twenty-four acres and employed six hundred people. Recently it had been razed to the ground, pending redevelopment: the usual suspects; homes, retail outlets, offices.

Uttoxeter was the point at which passengers changed for the Churnet Valley line through to Leek and Macclesfield. At one time there was also a train service to Ashbourne and Buxton. All of which gave the railway considerable presence at the bottom end of the town, though now merely two unstaffed platforms with shelters remain. In the past, race days at the neighbouring National Hunt course used to attract special excursions from across the midlands. Now, notwithstanding that the race course is at its zenith, no special steps are apparently taken to cater for the race crowds, and the image of large quantities of extra passengers attempting to cram aboard these single carriage trains is comical were it not so bizarre.

Leaving Longton

St Mary's,
Uttoxeter

The Weighing House

Market Street

The Dog & Partridge

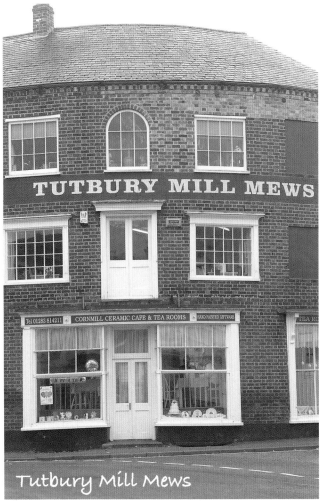

Tutbury Mill Mews

St Mary's, Tutbury

Thankfully it was not a race day and, alighting from the train, I put my money on the town to provide such entertainment as it could muster.

It was three o'clock and the carillon in the church steeple was playing as I walked up Bridge Street towards the market place. Too many cars went roaring past for me to be able to identify the tune, but it sounded incongruously like *The First Noel*. Shaped like a dumb bell – or a dog's bone for that matter – the Market Place plays host to its traditional activity on Wednesdays, Fridays and Saturdays, whilst there is additionally these days a Farmers' Market on the last Saturday in the month. They are all small but friendly affairs and attract a good deal of gossip-inclined custom from the town's rural hinterland.

At the top widening you come upon a curious little building built of stone. In the mists of time it was a weighing house, now it houses a newsagent. But its significance goes somewhat further, for it commemorates an act of penance on this spot in 1759, when Dr Samuel Johnson stood in the rain in contrite memory of the occasion that he refused to fill in for his indisposed father at the latter's Uttoxeter market bookstall.

The buildings which huddle round the Market Place date from a variety of periods and consist of an eclectic variety of styles. Quite a number of them are public houses of one sort or another which do well to continue in competition for what must be a demographically dwindling clientele. There are a good many cafés in the town too, which would suggest a voracious local appetite for pies and cakes and gossip. There were tempting pies on sale in the window of Sargeants butcher's shop, but on this occasion I managed to give temptation the slip.

Market Place becomes the pedestrianised High Street, or you can turn left into Carter Street, which I did because I intended to visit the Heritage Centre. Before I reached it, however, I paused to admire two quite different buildings: the United Reform Church, and a car showroom, of what I took to be 1930s origin, which reminded me evocatively of a toy garage I'd owned as a child. All that was missing was a row of old-fashioned petrol pumps beneath its curving forecourt.

The Heritage Centre is appropriately housed in a 17th Century cottage. There is no charge for admission, but it would be a hard-hearted individual who could leave without making a small donation. There are exhibitions of local history on two floors. Given that I had yet another train to catch I did them scant justice, but I did learn that when King Charles I and his retinue passed through the town on 24th May, 1645 they paid out five pounds and twelve shillings for peas and oats; that the town had once had a thriving brewery called Buntings whose premises occupied an extensive site behind the High Street which became The Maltings shopping precinct; and that the largest consignment of biscuits from Elkes factory was despatched by special train to Liverpool on 4th December 1935. Enough new facts for one day!

Two giggling girls were dismissive of the little train which arrived to take me on the last leg of my journey.

'Are they taking the mickey?' asked one out loud.

'It's like something out of *Thomas the Tank Engine*,' echoed her more literary-minded friend. I deduced they'd been to Alton Towers. Throughout the season there's a steady flow of youngsters who use the bus connection from Uttoxeter railway station to the UK's most popular theme park.

We pulled out past the race course, getting a good view of the back of the grandstand. Presently we were running alongside the River Dove. In a meadow a flock of sheep grazed, in the next a herd of Friesians. On the distant horizon I caught a glimpse of the bare, pointed tops of the Weaver Hills. In the opposite direction I caught sight of Trubshaw's picturesque 18th Century church at Marchington. Then, turning my head again, I saw Sudbury Hall. Never a dull moment if you know where to look!

Over a level crossing and then across the river – goodness, I'd inadvertently crossed the border into Derbyshire! Hanbury church and water tower atop the Needwood escarpment, somewhat crumpled thereabouts by the famous Fauld explosion. Scropton Crossing and its quaint signal cabin. Who remembers now that there was once a narrow gauge branch from here to the gypsum mines? And then, seeing Tutbury Castle on its hill, I knew it was time to get off.

The stimulating aroma of coffee emanated from Nestle's railwayside factory as I alighted, but I didn't linger to savour it, for my conscience urged me to get over the river and back into Staffordshire before anyone noticed my aberration. I'm old enough to remember the big mill which stood on the Staffordshire bank of the Dove. It crushed gypsum to make plaster. The ceiling of the Tower Ballroom in Blackpool was not least of its grateful recipients. A school friend and I once wrote to the manager requesting a visit to see its steam engine. He did us proud by return of post! We got to ride the mill's little Bristol-built Peckitt saddle tank across the trestle bridge which carried the railway over the Dove to join the main line. It was my first experience of the steam locomotive footplate and remains as precious to me as subsequent runs over the Settle & Carlisle and West Highland Extension in adulthood.

The mill closed in 1968 and was demolished a few years later, it is a picnic site now. Call that Progress if you dare. But I hadn't come to bury Tutbury, I'd come to praise it. For it is a lovely little town, smaller and more demure than Uttoxeter, and notable for its castle, its Norman church, its glassworks and its antiques centre. And like Uttoxeter, but *unlike* Burton-on-Trent, it has a museum, to which I repaired on the off chance it might be open.

Happily it was, and I was warmly received by a jaunty blonde lady of indeterminate age who insisted on showing me round personally. A single room suffices for all the town's rich history. And whilst, at a glance, you might think it little more than a load of junk, each item has its own intrinsic story to tell; furthermore, it must be said, my guide told it very well. In no particular order I was shown a Civil War cannon ball, a bust made out of glass for overnight storage of a wig, a mincer, a mangle, some Home Guard memorabilia, a mechanical device for producing hand signals through the passenger window of a motor car, several items essential for successful poaching forays, a collection of birds' eggs, a German machine gun from the First World War, a sewing machine, a typewriter, and various artefacts relating to Tutbury's glass and gypsum industries. I could not have been better entertained at the Science Museum or the Victoria & Albert. What thrilled me most was the discovery that Tutbury had been the location of a small business engaged in the production of flies for anglers. It had belonged to Roger Woolley, one of trout-fishing's acknowledged experts of the twentieth century. Though when I regaled my Father – a keen fly fisherman for a good proportion of his adult life – with this fascinating nugget of fishing lore, he couldn't remember ever having heard of Woolley, notwithstanding that he had resided within five miles of Woolley's premises for thirty years of his life.

I glanced at my watch. Bother! I was forty-nine years too late to catch the train back to Burton. Up until 11th June 1960, I could have completed my circular railway tour of Staffordshire by means of the Tutbury 'Jinny', a push & pull service which plied between Tutbury and Burton-on-Trent for over a century. It used to take ten minutes to do the journey by train. It takes twenty-three now by bus …

Walking Backwards 4

My old chum, Nick Spall, who used to dispense bacon butties, jokes and homespun wisdom in equal measure from a trailer at Uttoxeter railway station, appeared to have either overslept or moved on to fresh fields. An ex-squaddie, he would have been proud of my trek across Staffordshire, and would have sent me off laughing with a joke or two reverberating around my head for the rest of the day. In his absence, it was left to my own imagination to come up with anything amusing to say, but it seemed fast asleep as well.

It was the weather which was going to have the last laugh. Three dry days had ushered me from Kinver to Uttoxeter, how many more could I count on in what was proving to be a typically quixotic English summer? Isobel Lang had been optimistic with her televised weather forecast that morning, but then she has a naturally sunny disposition, so to speak, it is the lugubrious Rob McElwee that they usually wheel on when the news is bad.

The Staffordshire Way makes a McElweeian exit northwards from Uttoxeter, traversing an area cleared of old railway installations and given over now to car parking on race days. A pallet maker occupies part of the old condensed milk factory which stood alongside the platforms where the Churnet Valley trains once plied their trade. I thought I could detect, in a blue brick wall, the ghosts of an old platform.

September 9th was the date of the next race meeting being advertised on the grandstand on the far side of the railway. I wished the route of the Staffordshire Way had been equally well advertised. In the absence of visible waymarkers I referred to the map and trusted to my judgement. The first stile provided the first nettle sting of the day. What *is* it with nettles and stiles? Are they a metaphor for life's opportunities, in that they are invariably fraught with danger? A giant crane oversaw my progress across ungrazed meadows, more a landmark from afar for Uttoxeter now than the spire of its parish church.

The pioneers had contravened the spirit of the old Trade Descriptions Act when they had decided on the route to be essayed between Uttoxeter and Rocester, for throughout the majority of these five miles you find yourself walking in Derbyshire. There was no mistaking the point at which I would cross the River Dove, a procession of lorries on the A50 made that obvious, but there appeared to be dissension between the map and the guide book on one side and the waymarkers on the other. I think Health & Safety must have decided it was too risky for pedestrians to cross the A50, and I must say for once I was inclined to agree with them. Consequently, the accepted route now, is to cross the Dove by way of the modern road bridge, and then to pass beneath the dual-carriageway in a concrete culvert of the kind which invariably attracts graffiti artists of varying degrees of draughtsmanship and spelling ability. It is worth noting that the Tean has its confluence with the Dove at this point.

Marginalised by obsolescence, the old bridge consols itself in the thought that its replacement would never win any beauty competition. I leaned over one of its upstream cutwaters for a moment and watched some Mallard ducks paddling gamefully against the current. On the Staffordshire bank a pillbox stood ready to repel invaders from Derbyshire.

Derbyshire didn't appear any more interested in maintaining its public rights of way than its neighbour. I plodded across high-grassed fields of set-aside patrolled by irritating flies: even the demarcating fences had been allowed to fall derelict, the stiles redundant. I clambered up a bluff and was rewarded with a view back over the valley towards Uttoxeter, a view somewhat compromised by the teeming traffic on the dual-carriageway in the middle distance.

Now the Dove lay out of sight as I continued between Sidford Wood on one side and a big field of beans on the other. The pods were blackened and withered but the beans were green enough inside. Either the crop had caught some ghastly disease, or harvesting had been delayed. Perhaps the hiatus was a deliberate technique. Perhaps the whole of each plant would be mulched down and compressed into

Dove Bridge

some form of oil. Perhaps they were just *has* beans.

I hesitated by the entrance to Eaton Hall Farm, home of Doveridge Clay Sports & Corporate Lesiure. 'You are about to enter a shooting ground' proclaimed a notice, 'shooting is in progress when red flag flying'. Did the faded orange pennant fluttering half-heartedly on the gate constitute a red flag? I idly wondered. Furthermore the notice suggested that shooting commenced at ten. It was nine twenty-seven. I decided to get a move on. A few hundred yards on I encountered another notice: 'beware of falling clay fragments' … 'or FCFs to the cognoscenti,' I thought aloud.

A broad track hastened me away from the shooting zone. I passed through a nice new timber, five-bar gate which had been manufactured by A. J. Charlton of Buckland Down, Frome: Suppliers of Timber Gates By Appointment to Her Majesty. I was on the river plain, though the Dove itself was meandering its way southwards somewhere off-stage. Glancing back I saw that a big black cloud had its eye on me, and was licking its lips at the prospect of emptying itself all over me. In a neighbouring field, bales of hay wrapped in black plastic resembled giant rabbit droppings. Ahead, the Weaver Hills were little more than a grey smudge on the horizon. The farmhouse and outbuildings at Eaton Dovedale had been converted into prestigious housing. I could tell it was

prestigious by the light green paint scheme which had been adopted throughout. But just in case I was in any doubt, two prestigious dogs came out and barked at me to keep my distance.

The rain caught up with me at Sedsall, a derelict farm waiting its turn to be reinvented as prestigious housing. I might have been tempted to take shelter but a prominent notice board warned that trespassers entered at their own risk. Oddly enough it wasn't the rain on my clothes and exposed legs that proved uncomfortable, it was the soaking that the ground underfoot had taken, rapidly transferring its contents to my socks and shoes.

Drawing closely alongside the river, the path passed between musky clumps of Himalayan Balsam; alias Policeman's Helmet, alias Kiss Me on the Mountain. Prolific wildflower or pernicious weed? Opinions are divided. Personally I've witnessed the spread of this species along the watercourses beside which it thrives over twenty years. At first it appeared an attractive novelty. Now its seems a positive menace. It has come to define late summer beside rivers and canals, but like anything, you can have too much of it. Thank goodness its presence isn't felt all year.

The playing fields of Abbotsholme School offered some respite. The rugby posts were already erected pending a new season, and, as is the way with school XVs, new heroes. Someone – presumably the

Rocester Mill

groundsman – had a bonfire going upon which two lacrosse sticks had been sacrificed, an Abbotsholmian ritual perhaps? For one wild moment I felt like clambering onto the blaze and rescuing them, but then thought better of it, I would look peculiar walking along the Staffordshire Way with two lacrosse sticks protruding from my rucksack.

My feet were sodden, despite exaggerated attempts to lift them up. From a distance I must have looked like one of Mussolini's troops on the march. Eventually I reached the big red sandstone bridge which carries the old Roman Road from Derby to Rocester over the Dove. Gratefully, I sloshed back over the border into Staffordshire and found myself beside the entrance to the Hillsfield Ground of Rocester FC, or 'The Romans' to their legions of followers. Legions? Well the average home gate can be counted in double figures, but the club's proud history can be tentatively traced back to 1876 at least. Their first moment of glory, however, concerns the lifting of the Ashbourne News Cup against local rivals Ashbourne in 1913. An account in the *Uttoxeter Advertiser* of the day describes how the train packed with team and supporters arrived back at Rocester railway station and was met by throngs of cheering villagers. Hoisted shoulder high, the captain was carried through the streets in a procession led by Rocester Brass Band. In the restrained journalese of

the era, 'a night of merry making ensued'. These days, The Romans ply their trade in the Midland Football Alliance, and their fixtures take them to such exotic locations as Shifnal, Malvern, Coalville, Wednesfield, Barwell, Bridgnorth, Biddulph and Kirby Muxloe.

There can be few football teams in any league whose ground is juxtapositioned by so handsome a building as Tutbury Mill, erected at the behest of Richard Arkwright in 1781-2. Arkwright – as every schoolboy used to know – invented the spinning frame, a fact duly noted on a plaque beside the entrance to the mill. I had anticipated taking a photograph of the mill to illustrate these pages, but on arrival I found it shrouded in safety netting and scaffolding as, under the aegis of JCB, it is in the process of being refurbished as an engineering academy.

The next object of interest, as I progressed towards the village centre, was the Abbey Field. Sheep were grazing on a bumpy pasture which covered the foundations of an Augustinian abbey founded in 1141 and in existence until the Dissolution of the Monasteries in 1538. So much history in one small village! But there was more: a circular butter cross, millworkers cottages, churches of several denominations, and a second mill, of more traditional appearance, located alongside an arched bridge over the River Churnet. And I haven't even mentioned the *real* Romans and their impact on Rocester. But then, as Monty Python frequently asked, what did they do for us?

One thing's for sure, the Romans never played such an important role in Rocester as JCB. Joseph Cyril Bamford broke away from the family business after the Second World War. He sold his first trailer on Uttoxeter market for £345. But it was the development of the

Old railway bridge, Denstone

generic backhoe loader in 1953 which propelled JCB to the forefront of public perception and established the base of their worldwide development. The works at Rocester occupies over a hundred and seventy acres and is the company's World Headquarters, as evidenced by the regular flying in and out of helicopters conveying important guests and business associates. At ground level the plant's impact is mollified by a large landscaped lake which attracts a considerable variety of wildfowl. It attracts a considerable variety of humans as well: anglers, joggers, walkers, picnickers, feeders of birds, ice cream eaters, but not model boat enthusiasts, by some authoritarian reasoning they are banned from this wide sargasso inland sea. As I passed the entrance doors a man emerged in a suit carrying a briefcase. I recognised him immediately: he was my antithesis. He strode off towards the car park and his next appointment. I followed, buffeted by his slipstream, whistling *Linden Lea*.

I can recommend the breakfast rolls at Denstone Hall Farm Shop. I had one generously filled with bacon and egg accompanied by a cup of rather good black coffee. In between bites and sips I read *The Times* and ruminated. Since the official guide to the Staffordshire Way was last updated in 1996, the bottom end of the Churnet Valley Railway has been opened up for the use of walkers, cyclists and horse-riders between Denstone and Oakamoor. Thinking primarily of my still damp feet, I considered they stood more chance of drying out on the comparatively well-surfaced trackbed than on sodden field paths

and muddy farm tracks.

And so it came to pass that I departed from Denstone picturing myself with my legs stretched out and a compartment to myself. The former platforms (which once resounded to the pandemonium of boarders arriving with their trunks for a new term at Denstone College) remained intact to foster this illusion, and I soon found myself passing under a gracious overbridge built to last way beyond the railway age by navvies with an eye on immortality. Only the dripping trees broke the spell, no self-respecting team of plate-layers would have sanctioned such an uncontrolled spread of vegetation on their stretch of line.

The Churnet Valley Railway opened in 1849. Prior to that part of its route was occupied by the Uttoxeter extension of the Caldon Canal. Vestiges of this long lost waterway, though few and far between, can still be discerned if you penetrate the undergrowth. Winter would be a better time to go looking. Either side of Crumpwood Weir, where the canal once crossed the Churnet, can be found a bridge and a lock chamber. But with all this balsam about I hadn't a hope. I did, however, run the gauntlet of a nettlebed to cross the footbridge which spans the river immediately above the weir. Splendidly isolated, the house which stands here has been melancholically abandoned, its door and windows boarded up, its garden a riot of weeds save for some bravely flowering montbretia. Crossing the footbridge I came upon a little brick built sluice house at Quixhill, locked and deserted as if its boiler-suited and web-footed operatives had clocked off one day and never come back.

I returned to the railway and reboarded my private train. It puffed through a deep cutting and crossed the Churnet on a girder-built bridge. I lowered the window by means of a leather strap and waved at somnolent cattle in the watermeadows. A heron was hunched on the railing of a footbridge over the water, looking for a fish for his lunch. Like a silk scarf, smoke and steam wafted across the fields in the wake of the train. And then I blinked, for what appeared to be a Rhineland castle came into view, high above the line to the left. There was no alternative but to reach for the communication cord; penalty or no penalty.

Quixhill sluice gear

A daydream of course; the train that is, all the rest was very real. The castle, which must have drawn gasps of astonishment from passengers throughout the railway's existence, was built to the designs of Augustus Welby Northmore Pugin, for the 16th Earl of Shrewsbury, between 1847 and 1852. It looks like something out of *The Prisoner of Zenda* or *Gormenghast*, but if you approach it now you're likely to find it full of screaming children, for it has become a Catholic retreat for the young.

There are screams from the other side of the valley too, though not all issued by children. Hidden visually from the old railway line, but not aurally, Alton Towers is Britain's pre-eminent theme park, as the queues of cars which thread their way through

Alton village all summer long confirm. Somehow or other the village transcends this intrusion, being filled with handsome properties linked by a network of bewilderingly switchback streets.

I alighted at Alton station, as generations of pleasure-seeking excursionists had done before me. The elegant station buildings are surreally intact, and in the loving care of the Landmark Trust, an estimable organisation devoted to the rescue and subsequent holiday letting of some of Britain's most precious buildings. Rising steeply from a gate beside the station-master's house are a trio of aisles segregated by crush barriers once used for channelling crowds between the station and Alton Towers. Deserted and weedy now in an age where it's considered preferable to arrive by coach and car in a sad automotive procession that often stretches back as far as Denstone and beyond.

It was a steep climb from the station into Alton itself. There were odd overtones of Kinver. Another of Staffordshire's quasi Switzerlands I supposed.

Alton: crush barriers in the foreground, castle in the background

115

And plenty of bed & breakfast opportunities as befits a self-styled resort. I rejoined the Staffordshire Way proper by the Royal Oak and plunged into a bosky dingle which led to Toot Hill, a pocket of land looked after by the National Trust. I found myself catching up with a man walking a Jack Russell. With his bald head, elongated shorts and wellingtons he looked like a character out of *Teletubbies*. That made two of us.

The National Trust were right to requisition Toot Hill, it has all the ingredients of a magical landscape. I was admiring the bracken and the butterflies when I came upon the first drystone wall of my walk. Suddenly it occurred to me: 'I must have reached The North!' Time to lower my voice an octave and start wiping my nose with the back of my hand. An uneven path over protruding roots and occasional steps led almost vertically down to the banks of the Churnet. I looked back downstream to where the castle peeped above the trees, still looking positively Ruritanian.

If I had arrived a little later at the Rambler's Retreat I would have availed myself of afternoon tea. But it was still technically lunchtime and, judging by the number of vehicles in the car park, it was heaving inside. Dimmingsdale is a popular venue for postprandial strolls. Somewhere to walk off all the calories you've just acquired at the Rambler's Retreat. The area is delightfully scenic now, but was once a hive of industrial activity. Here stood an 18th Century

Breasting the hill, Greendale

smelting mill, an enterprise connected with the mining of ore at Ecton that I had learned about on my cycle ride through the Manifold Valley. The placid lakes encountered now were formerly reservoirs for the containment of waters used to power the machinery.

I passed an enviable residence called Earls Rock and took to a sandy track which ascended through a conifer plantation into a narrowing valley called Ousal Dale. It was a stiff climb and the sun had emerged to accentuate my labours. Eventually the track debauched on to a metalled lane and I saw a sign for a Youth Hostel at Longhurst Farm. Up above the tree line it was blowing a gale and the strange little bare plateau, over six hundred feet above sea level, resembled a monk's tonsure. In neighbouring fields, horses' manes were rippling in the wind. A succession of cattle grids brought me to the road which drops down through Stoney Dale to Oakamoor. Lined by crumbling mossy, lichened walls, it reeked of the resin of felled trees. I was only on it momentarily. Soon the waymarkers were leading me on a pebbly path through Sutton's Wood to Hawksmoor, climbing steeply again: a Beattock after Shap; a Rattery after Dainton.

Hawksmoor Nature Reserve is a two hundred and fifty acre woodland site cared for by the National Trust. The elaborate entrance was erected in 1933

Refreshment facility, Dimmingsdale

as a memorial to John Richard Beech Masefield, founder of the reserve and an individual credited by his appreciative peers with 'an unrivalled knowledge of the flora and fauna of his native county'. I was probably wondering about Mr Masefield when I took the wrong turn. But this was the fourth day of my walk across the county and I was beginning to develop a well-honed instinct for errors of my own making. The penny began to drop when the path I was on refused to let go of the road on the other side of the wall. A closer look at the map revealed I was heading in a south-westerly direction on one of the National Trust's paths instead of north-westwards on the Staffordshire Way. Shamefacedly I retraced my steps, hoping that no one had seen my about turn.

The correct route lay down a broad and steeply descending lane through mixed woodland, picturesquely dappled now that the sun had gained ascendency over the cloud. The guide book informed me that the stunted oaks to my left and right were a legacy of charcoal burning and tanning. Eventually I emerged from the woods at East Wall Farm, a delightful collection of redbrick farm buildings overlooking a large duckpond.

At this point I was intrigued by the guide book's reference to earthworks remaining from the tramway which had linked Woodhead Colliery with the Caldon Canal – you will recall me mentioning it on

East Wall Farm

my bicycle ride. Unfortunately the next section of the Staffordshire Way lay alongside the Churnet whose damp water meadows were proving an ideal environment for the propagation of what I now regarded as my implacable enemy – Himalayan Balsam. It had summoned up its henchmen, thistles and nettles, and, given the muddy nature of the waterside path, I spent the next quarter of an hour uncomfortably thrashing about with the dual purpose of keeping to the route and avoiding being stung.

By the time I emerged from this jungle, into a fairly respectable field, I had forgotten all about the old tramway. As I gratefully heaved myself across the stile, a young, red-headed woman came jauntily down the hillside towards me, obviously intent in going the way I had come. Like me she was wearing shorts … or so I thought!

'It's terrible back there,' I warned her. 'Have you been through recently?'

'Not for a few months,' she admitted, in an unexpected contralto.

'Well watch out for the nettles and thistles,' I advised. 'It's awful if you've got shorts on.'

'Oh these roll down,' she said blithely as we went our separate ways: she, no doubt, wondering at the inadequate preparation endemic in middle-aged men; me pondering on the wonders of modern outdoor gear.

Somewhere up the ensuing hillside I took an incorrect turn and arrived at Kingsley Holt from the wrong direction, but the error was of little consequence. Soon I was reunited with the Staffordshire Way by the Methodist church and found my route along an alley between two houses. In the driveway of one of these houses, a man was admitting – to the obvious incredulity of his neighbour – that he had never been to Ipstones Show. Beyond the alley, the path stretched obviously ahead through fields. Peeping above the wooded valley was a tall brick chimney that I imagined belonged to Bolton's copper works.

I came to a field filled with Friesians and had to pick my way gingerly between cowpats. Three-quarters of the way across the field I reached an electric fence. No provision had been made for walkers, so I sort of limbo-danced my way beneath it, deciding that I would prefer the upper part of my abdomen to be electrocuted as opposed to the lower. The reason for the electric fence became apparent as I breasted the rise, for there lay a Charolais bull, obliviously resting from his labours. You can imagine how grateful I was to put that particular field behind me: to be electrocuted was forgivable, to be electrocuted *and* gored would smack of carelessness.

The path emerged from its agricultural excesses by Kingsley's war memorial. I crossed the A52 and went through a kissing-gate into the churchyard which contained some imposing upright gravestones from the 19th Century. Somehow or other I contrived to leave the churchyard by the wrong path yet again – three wrong turns in one afternoon: I was losing my grip! But once more I was let off lightly, and found my way back magnetically onto the correct route at the far end of the village.

There were fine views across the valley towards the Staffordshire Moorlands: Ipstones church could be descried at 11 o'clock; Foxt at 1. Entering a wood at the foot of a field I found the descent steepening as the Staffordshire Way skirted the perimeter fencing of the Kingsley Bird & Falconry Centre. The precipitous – not to say treacherous – nature of the path down into the Churnet Valley emphasised its depth at this point. I duly slipped and slithered downwards, coming to an abrupt halt where a bridge carried the Churnet Valley Railway over the river. Unlike the section of the railway I had walked along earlier in the day, this part retains its tracks – or at least one of them – and carries preserved trains, which shuttle up and down the valley between Leekbrook and Froghall; though, being a Thursday, I didn't expect to see any.

Having crossed the river itself on a slender footbridge, I followed the path up to the Caldon Canal and turned left. I hadn't gone very far when I came upon a milepost, very much in the same style as those I had encountered on the Trent & Mersey Canal in the vicinity of Shugborough. This is not entirely surprising, for the Caldon Canal was a branch of the Trent & Mersey and the original mileposts were also cast by Rangeley & Dixon of Stone. This one bore the inscription: Etruria 16, Uttoxeter 14, and was a replica put up by the Caldon Canal Society in 1983. It had been unveiled by Earl Ferrers, Minister of State for Agriculture, Fisheries and Food, and sponsored by the Midland Bank: how quickly officials are forgotten; how swiftly banks go out of business. Alongside the cast iron milepost stood an even older stone example, its figures reading 16 and 1 respectively; no, they hadn't discovered a short cut, 1 informed the distance to Froghall before the Uttoxeter extension was opened in 1811.

River, canal and railway progress arm in arm up the narrow, bosky valley. It might occur to you to wonder why they went to the trouble of providing the two man-made methods of transport through such an apparently remote area. The answer is that the Churnet Valley wasn't always so bucolic. Iron ore and limestone were once extensively mined in the district. In the middle of the 19th Century upwards of thirty boats a day were conveying ore along the canal. For some curious reason, the canal – pretty as it is now – doesn't attract pleasure boats in such high numbers. Even in the middle of August, I saw only a handful of boats moving. Bridge 53 is well known in canal circles, both for its oddly pointed arch, and its nickname: 'Cherry Eye Bridge'. It is said that the name was derived from the invariably inflamed and bloodshot eyes of the local iron workers.

Rounding a sharp bend I came upon a spill weir upon which a yellow wagtail was searching assiduously for grubs. The towpath changed sides at Bridge 52. An interpretive board explained the technique employed by boat captains to ensure that the towing rope didn't get snagged when the horse had to change sides in days gone by. I came upon a lock overlooked by the shell of an old flint mill. The adjoining house was up for sale. I idly wondered if I could count on winning the lottery that week.

Not expecting to see any trains go by, I was pleasantly surprised to hear a diesel horn echoing through the woods, and I hadn't walked much further before a locomotive came clattering along the line, chuntering away to itself. I would be doing my railway

The Black Lion, Consall Forge

119

The Caldon Canal at Consall

The Churnet Valley Railway

readers a disservice were I not to give them the number. It was 37075, a 47 year old English Electric veteran of such disparate depots as Thornaby, Tinsley and March. How did it feel pottering up and down the Churnet Valley at twenty-five miles an hour when it had once sped under East Anglian skies with expresses to Kings Lynn? At least it had been spared the breaker's torch, and I was sure the three young men I spotted in its cab as it went by – and who wouldn't have even been born when it was built in Darlington in 1962 – regarded this inanimate lump of metal with something approaching love.

All of which brought me to Consall Forge, and another labour of love, the restored station. How holistic it looked in this wooded cleft in the hills. No road could have managed such affinity with its setting. In fact the nice thing about Consall Forge is that no road reaches it at all, not officially at any rate. So the congenial Black Lion (which recently revived the tradition of having barrels of beer delivered by train) has to rely on walkers, boaters and railway passengers for its custom, which pretty much automatically filters out the riffraff, you might say.

For about a mile upstream of Consall Forge, river and canal join forces, which brought to mind the similar arrangement at Alrewas that I discovered on my bicycle ride. James Brindley surveyed the Caldon Canal but caught a chill in doing so which resulted in his death. At the deliciously remote Oakmeadow Ford Lock, the two watercourses resume their independence. A notice warns boaters not to proceed downstream if the river level is above a certain point on a gauge at the tail of the lock.

There are items of interest wherever one looks in Cheddleton. The station is the headquarters of the group who operate the Churnet Valley Railway and their collection of motive power and rolling stock can be seen and admired from the Staffordshire Way. They offer refreshments too at their Grade II listed station, a charming little Tudor structure attributed to William Sugden, who we met previously on board *Deli*. On this occasion, and as my day's walk was drawing to a close, I kept to the Staffordshire Way which follows the towpath up through a pair of locks to where Cheddleton Flint Mill stands demurely down below the level of the canal. In my opinion this is one of the great little museums of England, and if its opening hours are as unfathomable as its machinery, to my way of thinking this only adds to its charm. Needless to say, it was closed.

Cheddleton Flint Mill

Blackie at Hints Ford

Gailey Round House

Roman remains, Wall

LVS 184

Wall Roman Town

By-roads

ANGELA Johnson trundled along Watling Street accompanied by two fifty-somethings: Blackie, her Austin A30, churned off the Longbridge production line in 1952; and me, churned off the strikingly less prolific Pearsons of Paisley production line in exactly the same year. Both quinquagenarians were behaving themselves, thus far. The plan was to follow as much of Watling Street's progress through Staffordshire as possible, without tweaking Warwickshire or Shropshire, and then to explore the rabbit-warren of by-roads which characterise the remote western marches of the county.

At the age of eight I lived, quite literally, within a stone's throw of Watling Street where it nudged Leicestershire. The traffic was audible, if less processional than now. The euphony of the road's name appealed to my burgeoning grasp of topography. Vaguely, I imagined its course, its extremities. Erroneously, I was told it went to Holyhead, which I confused with Hollywood. Variously, the other end was deemed to be London or Dover. Facts, in common with statistics, are not always to be relied upon. Imagination is invariably a better disciple.

Solely the most disingenuous of travel writers – or someone hired at great expense to put on a bold PR front – would pretend that Staffordshire is without its uglier places. Indeed, it sometimes seems to me that, notwithstanding the battalions of planners and schemers at our disposal, we have a well-honed capacity for making it even uglier as we go along; signage being a particular culprit. And by most tenets, Fazeley – in the bottom right hand corner of the county – is as ugly as they come. But before we took to the road we elected to enjoy a whistle-stop tour of Fazeley's attractions which didn't, as far as two middle-aged people and a veteran motor car were concerned, include the siren call of Drayton Manor Theme Park; Thomas the Tank Engine notwithstanding.

Fazeley itself is not most people's idea of a playground, but most industrial archaeologists would view it as one. They would relish its status as a canal junction, they would be in awe of its mills, its workers cottages, the orange brick United Methodist Free Church of 1884, the terracotta Parish Hall of 1897, why even the timber yard with its gargantuan crane would inspire affection.

The smaller, more self-effacing of the two canalside mills dates from 1790. It belonged to Sir Robert Peel, father of the Prime Minister of the same name. But the mill you can't miss, Tolson's Mill, which towers over Watling Street like an escapee from Bolton or Oldham, is of late 19th Century origin. Within its five towering storeys its workforce beavered way in the production of haberdashery and upholstery. And when they weren't beavering away at work, they ran their own concert band, delightfully known as Tolson's Music Weavers. Both mills now house an agglomeration of light, and for the most part inscrutable, industries.

To harmonise with the age of our vehicle, I had three old one inch Ordnance Survey maps dating from just after the end of the Second World War with me, along with a copy of Henry Thorold's *Shell Guide to Staffordshire*, itself a now dated gazetteer of 1978. Fazeley is, strictly speaking, not even on the A5 anymore, for that number belongs to a dual-carriageway which by-passes it to the north nowadays. Nevertheless there remained a good deal of traffic on the old Roman Road if our departure was anything to go by, and we trundled out of Fazeley in a line of cars, vans and lorries as lumbering as the elephants in Jolly's Circus, whose effulgent red and yellow big top was prominent in a field on the outskirts.

Beyond Bonehill we happily spurned the opportunity to join the new A5, remaining unwaveringly on the old road, content not to join the Gadarene swine, snaking up the neighbouring hillside in a hurry to get to goodness knows where. The old road was apologetically empty, save for the occasional quarry lorry. On either side lay polytunnels and pick your own fruit farms. Dozens of times I had driven along this section of the Watling Street, and never given so much as a passing thought to the peculiarly named village of Hints. Now, in an old car, at a sedate pace, it seemed churlish not to tarry.

'Let's try the next left,' I suggested to Angela who wasn't to know I'd seen the irresistible word 'ford' inscribed on the map. She leaned over and turned a knob beneath the centre of the windscreen and, in wonderfully quaint fashion, an illuminated semaphore indicator flicked out to the horizontal between the doors on the passenger side.

We discovered that there is more to Hints than meets the eye. In fact you could say that there was little hint of what lay down the lane signposted discouragingly as a No Through Road. Initially, smug barn conversions were suggestive of a well-heeled desire for privacy, but we persisted and came upon a pretty little Victorian church with a bell-cote, before taking another fork which led to Bourne Brook and the ford. In the wake of weeks of rain, the flow was disappointing, but the ford itself reminded me forcibly of the one at Butterton that I had encountered on my bike ride, in so much that the lane and watercourse ran one upon the other for perhaps the length of a cricket wicket, as opposed to merely crossing each other at right angles.

I could sense that Henry Thorold had also been smitten by Hints: he alluded to a hall that had been demolished after the Second World War, though it was still indicated on my map of 1947; he suggested that the etymology might have Welsh origins; but he failed to refer to Gold's Clump and its Roman – or possibly even older – tumulus, or the discovery by labourers, digging on the heights of Hints Common in 1792, of a lead ingot bearing a Roman inscription precisely dating it to 76AD, which now resides in Tamworth Castle. But the story I like most about Hints concerns the establishment of a zoo there in 1954 by two rival pet shop proprietors from Sutton Coldfield, Molly Badham and Nathalie Evans. The womens' particular speciality was chimpanzees and they trained the famous chimps who starred in the Brooke Bond PG Tips tea advertising campaign that so caught the viewing public's imagination in the 'sixties and 'seventies. In the end, Hints Zoo outgrew its location, and Molly and Natalie moved to a site in neighbouring Leicestershire where they established Twycross Zoo.

We joined the A5 proper at Weeford, but were soon going off at a tangent again, for it would have been careless of us not to call in at Wall and see what remained of the old Roman settlement of Letocetum. Indeed, it was scandalous that I had lived for the best part of half a century within a dozen miles of Wall and never visited it. But then, what's the odd fifty years in the face of two thousand!

We left our chariot in the car park and ambled up the old line of Watling Street predating the present dual-carriageway. Devoid of traffic, devoid of Romans, Wall resembled an ancient villager, drawn up by the fireside and dwelling on the past. We squeezed through an alleyway between a privet hedge and a wooden fence and found ourselves in an area of open ground rising towards a small church. The scene would have been otherwise unremarkable but for a series of foundation walls accompanied by squat interpretive boards. From these we gleaned something of Letocetum's role in the scheme of things during the 1st Century. It seemed that the settlement's main purpose was to provide lodging and refreshment facilities for travellers along the Roman Road, in essence an early forerunner of a motorway service area. We couldn't help wondering if the toilets had been equally depressing and the food just as bland. In what remained of the Exercise Hall we came upon an illustration of half-dressed men wrestling, obviously the supporters of

Maer Hills
Dorothy Clive Garden
Maer
Sidway
Standon
Pumping Station
Millmeece
M6
Slindon
Sugnall
Cop Mere
Eccleshall
High Offley
Anchor Inn
Norbury Junction
Gnosall
Shropshire Union Canal
Stafford
Orslow Brineton
Watling Street
Gailey
aqueduct
Round House
Cannock Chase
Cannock
A5
Chasewater
Lichfield
Weston under Lizard
M6 Toll
Wall
North
Brownhills
Tamworth
Hints
Fazeley

Cornoviorum (or Wroxeter) FC on the way back from defeat at the hands of a Londinium club.

Sometimes you're reluctant to leave the past behind, sometimes you can't wait to escape. I think on this occasion both Angela and I were glad to get back into Blackie's red leather interior and resume our travelling. Not for the first time I automatically reached for the seat belt, much to Angela's amusement, cars of a certain age not being required by law to be so fitted.

With many a zig and many a zag, we rejoined the A5 at Muckley Corner. With more time at our disposal we would have probably gone and had a look at the canal reservoir at Chasewater and watched the steam trains which trundle round two-thirds of its circumference upon former colliery tracks, but with a top speed of thirty-five miles per hour, we were going to have to be selective with the places where we stopped. At regular intervals, when the coast was clear, Angela would thrust her right arm out of the window and wave on the traffic which had gathered behind us. They didn't always appear in a hurry to pass. Either they were being ultra-cautious, or they just enjoyed travelling behind so delightful a vehicle.

At Bridgtown – an outpost of Cannock – we successfully untangled a cats cradle of roads, passed the gherkin-like Ramada Hotel at Lion Point, and forged on through a nebulous zone of retail parks before coming to Four Crosses and fresh air. Here, the landlord of the local pub had made something of a celebrity of himself by offering 'recession-busting' bar meals for a pound. Sadly it was a little too early in the day to sample his largesse. A mile or two further on we caught glittering glimpses through a mask of woodland of some canal reservoirs, crossed the M6 motorway, and pulled up at Gailey Round House, an enchanting little shop overlooking a lock on the Staffordshire & Worcestershire Canal.

The round house was erected circa 1771 to both house the lock-keeper and his family and to provide him with an elevated view over the flight of locks leading down towards Penkridge. That over two hundred years later it still plays a role in the life of the canal is somehow most satisfying. Having known Eileen Lester, the proprietress of the canal shop, and her daughter, Karen, for the best part of thirty years, I thought it only right to introduce Angela and her A30. Eileen was so excited she left the till open. Furthermore, I was soon experiencing the fate of lone males everywhere in the company of two members of the opposite sex, that of not being

able to get a word in edgeways.

Angela was much taken by the round house – Eileen's home as well as her place of work – and the charm of its canal setting. Blackie was much taken with a Ford Anglia parked by the gate of a canalside cottage. Trade was slow, Eileen was explaining, on account of the Shebdon Breach. Had I left them gossiping any longer, they'd have probably discovered they were related. In the event I managed to tear Angela away before Eileen embarked on her favourite Michael Pearson story, the one about lock-working being like your first kiss …

Beyond Gailey roundabout and the A5's intersection with the main road between Wolverhampton and Stafford, we found ourselves out in open countryside for practically the first time, crossing the River Penk where the map revealed there had once been a watermill, and passing the Bell Inn, charmingly self-proclaimed as a 'Noted Ham 'n Eggery'. Then we went under the Shropshire Union Canal, or rather Thomas Telford's Birmingham & Liverpool Junction Canal of 1835, the last great main line of the Canal Age which, you will remember I had already walked across when following the Staffordshire Way. Angela, for her part – and though

The Ramada Hotel, Bridgtown

she'd been familiar with the A5 since childhood holidays in North Wales – had always assumed that Stretton Aqueduct carried a *railway*.

'I always thought it was one of those lines thingy had closed, you know, what's his name? … Johnny hates him.'

Johnny is Angela's husband, by all accounts a dead-ringer for the late Sid James, hence the slogan on the side of his window-fitting business's van: 'Carry on Glazing'.

'Johnny and I would obviously have a good deal in common,' I replied. 'And I can hardly bring myself to mention the culprit's name, but just for the record it was Beeching.'

'That's the one,' laughed Angela; not that it was a joking matter. 'Johnny's dad was a driver out of Snow Hill,' she continued, cementing my admiration for a man I'd never met even further.

A lengthy stone-built wall led to the imposing entrance to Weston Park. But stately homes were not part of our itinerary, and, aware that just over a mile away stood the county boundary with Shropshire, I indicated to Angela that we should turn sharp right. She had the good sense to wait until there was a gap in the oncoming traffic.

It was as if a wand had been waved. We could almost hear Blackie sigh with relief. For the next six or seven miles we proceeded sedately along muddy, tractor-stained lanes winding between farmland. Place names read like a roll call:

'Blymhill?'

'Here sir.'

'Brineton?'

'Here sir.'

'Chatwell?'

'Here sir.'

'Orslow?'

'Here sir.'

'Goosemoor?'

…

'Where the devil's Goosemoor?'

'Expelled, sir.'

'Oh yes, following that unfortunate incident with Matron.'

We began to collect herds of Holstein Friesians: the Orslow Herd, the Malberry Herd, the Cowley Herd. Trails of cowpats crossed the road at strategic intervals. A buzzard, bursting out of the hedgrow like a bankrobber, almost took the roof off the car. On the outskirts of Gnosall we encountered the canal again, passing this time more conventionally above it.

Gnosall reminded me of that old comic song by Flanders and Swann about The Gnu. Only you don't say 'Ger-no-sall, you say 'No-zull'. Staffordshire's 'Millennium Way' passes through Gnosall, employing hereabouts the trackbed of the old Wellington to Stafford railway line to stay traffic-free on its forty mile journey between Newport and Burton-on-Trent. Beechinged out of existence, the line had been opened in 1849 by the Shropshire Union Railways & Canal Co. Few of its shareholders then would have envisaged the canal which ran through Gnosall outliving the new-fangled railway.

St Lawrence's, Gnosall

Norbury Junction

Gnosall has a notable church, but we left that for another day, and motored along more country lanes to the old canal community of Norbury Junction, in doing so, passing twice beneath Shelmore Great Bank which had almost been Telford's undoing. Six years in the making, this huge earthwork – a mile long and sixty feet high – need not have been erected at all if Lord Anson of Norbury Park had not stubbornly refused to have his pheasant-rearing reserves disturbed. Time after time the bank's unstable spoil slipped. In fading health, Telford agreed to the proposal that William Cubitt – who later went on to make his name as a railway builder – should deputise for him as the canal company's engineer. Telford visited the works in March 1834 and Cubitt took him on a conducted tour. Frail and deaf, the great engineer regarded the embankment which had caused considerable delay and extra expense in completing the canal. One can imagine the young Cubitt confidently reassuring his elderly companion, but a few weeks after Telford's visit, Shelmore slipped again, and by the time Telford died on 2nd September 1834 his last canal remained uncompleted. Not until the following January was the bank considered strong enough to fill the canal for the first boat to cross.

Norbury became a canal junction with the almost simultaneous completion of a branch canal to Newport connecting with the Shrewsbury Canal and the intriguingly titled Shropshire Tub Boat Canals. Sadly, all those canals were abandoned by the LMS Railway Co. during the Second World War – when presumably everyone who cared about keeping canals open had their backs turned. The long ladder of locks which led inexorably down to the Weald Moors, has long since been exorcised from the landscape, but Norbury proudly clings on to its suffix and remains a popular canal location, attracting boaters, walkers and motorists alike by virtue of its pub, café and boatyard.

Down high-hedged, brackeny lanes, we slipped through Norbury itself, ignoring Thorold's tacit invitation to admire the church's effigy of a cross-legged knight. We zigzagged across the busy Newport to Newcastle-under-Lyme highway and passed Loynton Farm, home to an eponymous flock of Jacob sheep. Pears hung bountifully over the high wall of Loynton Hall. Blackie chugged on, totally in tune with her surroundings. Round the next bend we braked and swerved, simply to avoid two magpies, a pheasant and a wood pigeon enjoying a mid-road tittle-tattle.

By roads so rustic and unkempt that it was hard to credit that we were still on the Queen's Highway, we chanced ('not merely by chance') upon the Anchor Inn, canalside beneath the hummock upon which High Offley stands. I make no excuse for a second literary pilgrimage to The Anchor. It previously played a cameo role in *Me, My Morgan, and the*

A floral Anchor Inn

Midlands, but that was not sufficient excuse for me to ignore it on this occcasion. Besides, I felt an almost proprietorial obligation to show it off to Angela.

They say that The Anchor is a contemporary of the canal's, which certainly rings true, otherwise why would it be where it is, out in the middle of nowhere? In truth it looks more like a modest villa of the early Victorian era than a pub. At one time it was called The Sebastopol after the battle in the Crimean War, and the origin of its present name is shrouded in a beery haze; anchors hardly being the stuff of narrow boats. On warm days you can sit out in the garden and peep over the privet hedge at the cabin tops of passing boats. But, pleasant a pastime as this may be, it has always seemed to me to be a waste not to remain in the bar, with its tiled floor and high-backed settles, listening to the ticking of the grandfather clock. After all one can sit in a beer garden any time, time capsules themselves are somewhat rarer. The pub has been in the same family since 1870, and the landlady follows her forebears footsteps each time she descends to the cellar to refill her jug of ale from the barrel. The only surprise is that the ale in question comes all the way from Wiltshire. Oh that it came by canal boat!

It was a minute short of noon and we arrived just in time to hear the bolts being drawn. A man fitting a tow bar to a car stood up to admire Blackie. He was the landlady's, daughter's partner, he

The real Anchor Inn

explained, and he was glad to see us, trade having been all but absent since the Shebdon Breach. Something of an authority on the subject by now, I was able to let him into the secret surrounding the Portugese clay. I wondered aloud if there would be any chance of compensation for canalside businesses? He wasn't banking on it!

A heavenly pint of 6X for me, a half of shandy for Angela, with cheese sandwiches to follow in their own good time; which at The Anchor gives every indication of being endless. It was Angela's preference to take our drinks out into the garden where, presently, we were joined by two walkers; quite a crowd in the circumstances. When our sandwiches were ready, the landlady kindly recommended we eat them inside, so as to avoid the wasps; she had been stung the week before. Poor dear, last time I'd called in she'd had toothache!

Back inside, we set about our sandwiches, pausing only to comment on this or that aspect of the décor. With her woman's eye, Angela was mentally re-arranging things, she whisperingly confided. With my male eye I wouldn't have altered a thing, pubs like this are too precious to fiddle with, any forelock tug to Progress being anathema.

Beyond The Anchor – perhaps even beyond time itself – we lost ourselves on the watershed which indiscriminatingly separates the drops of rain that find themselves trickling westwards to join the Severn, and those that find their way into the Trent. Not lost in the sense that we didn't know where we were, I hasten to add, but rather more agreeably lost in the sense that the modern world would have been hard pressed to find us, puttering along at twenty miles per hour, a soft breeze blowing through the quarter lights, the flying silver A on the bonnet glinting in the sunshine. We crossed a tiny watercourse which the map referred to as Lonco Brook. There was a mill marked on my old map, but whatever remained of it was hidden at the end of a drive protected by high security gates.

Skirting the tempting (but not *that* tempting) little town of Eccleshall to the west, we came to Cop Mere, hidden from public gaze by a belt of trees. Often it occurs to me, trees can be too much of a good thing. The River Sow – last encountered, you'll hopefully recall, on my train ride around the county, in a park in Stafford – pours into one end of Cop Mere and emerges out of the other. Only anglers are afforded intimacy with the setting. Three-quarters of a mile upstream the Sow was once harnessed to drive the machinery of Walkmill. Semi-derelict now – though there are signs that someone has been working to

refurbish it – the mill once dealt in woollen cloths, its very name deriving from the practice of fulling or 'walking'. Later it ground corn. We pulled in for a moment by the reedy mill pond, melancholically disposed towards the general air of neglect and decay. Oddly, in such a state of undress, the mill (bearing the date of its construction – 1830) seemed more redolent of its working days than if it had been successfully converted into the desirable dwelling which I could sense Angela was picturing. I would not have batted an eyelid if the miller had emerged with a sack of freshly ground meal over his dusty shoulder.

In motion again and more names to conjure with: Sugnall, Brockton and Slindon. Said out loud in sequence they sounded like a veterinary practice; as well they might have been, out in these agricultural wilds. A flock of seagulls had taken possession of a freshly ploughed field. They always remind me of Vikings, these maritime interlopers, uncouth invaders of the countryside.

'Steaming Today' announced a sign at Mill Meece, a beguiling offer by any standards. If Angela was better placed to resist, she was too polite to say so. We pulled into a field overlooking the railway and parted with some money at the gate.

'Quickly,' urged a man in a red boiler suit. 'We're just changing over the engines. Follow the signs …'

The engines in question were known as 'the Gentle Giants', a pair of massive horizontal steam engines which spent over a hundred years between them drawing water out of underground boreholes in the valley of Izaak Walton's Meece to supply The Potteries with water for home and industry. By the time we'd found our way round the back of the building, an excited little knot of acolytes was gathered between the two behemoths, and our friend in the red boiler suit – whose tongue had the air of County Durham about it – had purloined a young boy to apply the brake to the machine on the left, supplied by Ashton Frost of Blackburn in 1914.

I hoped the boy would remember the treat for the rest of his days, it was like visiting the circus and being asked to tame a lion. Its huge flywheel stilled, attention turned to its neighbour, a Hathorn Davey of Leeds, twelve years the junior of the Ashton Frost.

'I'm just going to start the barring engine,' announced our friend. 'That'll start the flywheel going, before the big engine kicks in.' The barring engine, I noticed, had been made by Marshalls of Gainsborough; I see no devils in such details, only angels.

In fact a couple of false starts ensued, accompanied

Mill Meece

by some good natured banter amongst the cognoscenti; pump enthusiasts to a man. But then the younger of the Gentle Giants slowly eased itself into action, and the audience stood back in admiration, hypnotised by the nineteen revs per minute of the nineteen foot, six inch flywheel; no orator could have held us more firmly in his grip. From an adjacent panel I learned that the engine had been installed by one Harry Cusworth in 1926. It took him the best part of a year. The engine had arrived as a kit of parts at Standon Bridge station, just up the road. With the help of two brawny farm labourers and a horse and cart, Harry had manhandled the parts down to the pumping station. I was not surprised to learn that some difficulty had been experienced in getting the flywheel through the engine house door, even though it had been supplied in two pieces. Installing the new steam engine hadn't been Harry's only activity during his period of employment at Mill Meece. In due course his expectant wife chose to go south for her confinement. As the date of the birth approached, he took leave to visit her, only to receive a telegram threatening dismissal. It is good to record that he called his employer's bluff and stayed on for the birth, predicting quite rightly that they would have more trouble finding a suitable replacement than

Standon Mill

allowing him an extra day or two with his new daughter!

Back out in the open air there were a good many side shows, so to speak: old cars, motorcycles, tractors and model steam engines. Indeed, it occurred to us that, with advance warning, we could have entered Blackie as an exhibit. I was amused by the men exhibiting pumps; though not, I hasten to add, in a derogatory way. It just seems such a gentle hobby, to draw up a deckchair and listen to the chuntering of an array of Listers, whilst basking in the admiration and envy of fellow enthusiasts. If only some of history's despots had taken up pump restoration and exhibiting, the world might have been a safer and more contented place.

The hundred tons or so of coal a day required to feed the massive trio of boilers at Mill Meece Pumping Station would, I imagined, but neglected unprofessionally to ask, have arrived in railway wagons at Standon Bridge station and been carried down the road – just like the Hathorn Davey – by horse and cart. The station closed the year Blackie and I were built, but, as is often the case, there is still a coal merchant in what remains of the old goods yard. Nowadays you can lean over the stone parapets of the station bridge and watch Sir Richard Branson's sleek silver Pendolinos whoosh beneath you at a hundred and twenty-five miles per hour, scarcely registering that there was once a station here at all.

Beyond the railway bridge we came upon the delightful surprise of a working animal feeds mill housed in traditional mill buildings. Thorold notes that Gilbert Scott rebuilt Standon's church in 1846. We pictured him stepping from a stopping train on Joseph Locke's recently completed Grand Junction Line. As Standon's station closed so did Whitmore, three miles up the line. It was from Whitmore station in 1839 that Charles Darwin and his bride Emma Wedgwood left for London, having been married in St Peter's church at Maer.

Maer was our next port of call, a pretty estate village tucked in folds of the Maer Hills which rise to 700ft to the north. Charles Darwin was a frequent visitor to Maer, for he particularly enjoyed the company of his uncle, Josiah Wedgwood II, and it was perhaps not that unnatural that he should additionally fall in love with his cousin. The Darwins and the Wedgwood's had, after all, enjoyed a close association since Josiah Wedgwood and Erasmus Darwin had become firm friends and business associates in the 1770s. Josiah's first daughter, Susannah, had already married Robert Darwin, Charles' father.

Maer Hall itself dates from *circa* 1680, and overlooks a mere from which its name was derived. The mere forms the source of the River Tern, which flows in a wide arc to meet the Severn near

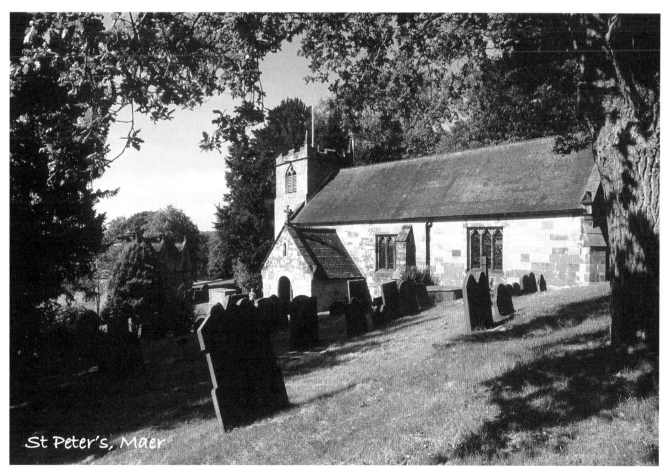

St Peter's, Maer

Shrewsbury. In the 18th Century the grounds were landscaped by Capability Brown. The hall was acquired by Josiah Wedgwood II in 1802 with capital borrowed from his brother-in-law, Robert Darwin. Along with the gracious setting, part of its attraction must have been that it lay just seven miles west of the Wedgwood pottery at Etruria.

It was apparently Josiah Wedgwood II who persuaded a doubtful Robert Darwin to permit his son to join the scientific expedition aboard HMS *Beagle*. Furthermore, there is some suggestion that some of the work which eventually appeared in his seminal *On the Origin of Species* was gathered in the relaxed atmosphere prevalent at Maer, during

Dorothy Clive Garden

some of it occupying the site of a worked-out gravel quarry which lends it considerable vertical drama. The garden was begun in 1940 by Colonel Harry Clive as somewhere for his wife Dorothy, who suffered from Parkinson's disease, to find exercise and solace in equal measure. Unfortunately Dorothy died within a couple of years of work on the garden commencing, but her husband went on with developing the site in her memory, later forming a trust to maintain the garden for posterity after his own death.

Though, judging from the car park, the grounds were playing host to a good number of visitors – not least a coach party from Nottingham – the garden quickly swallowed Angela

Darwin's frequent stays there. But the story I like best about Darwin is that he sat down one day and drew up a list of the pros and cons of getting married. Amongst the pros was the thought that a wife would be 'better than a dog' in terms of companionship. Amongst the cons was the fear that he would have less money to spend on books; a man after my own bibliophilic heart! Incidentally, on sale in St Peter's Church are delightful tea towels bearing the inscription: 'better than a dog'; a useful reminder for males who number washing and drying of dishes amongst their many marital duties.

We turned left onto the A51 opposite Maer's war memorial. Woodland masked Berth Hill, the site of an Iron Age fort. We were running out of afternoon, and we were running out of Staffordshire. A mile short of the Shropshire border it seemed sensible to terminate our journey amidst the horticultural splendour of the Dorothy Clive Garden. 'Woven into the tapestry of the magnificent Staffordshire countryside' – in the lurid prose of the brochure – it was certainly a far cry from Fazeley.

'Nice car,' said the man at the gate, with an admiring glance at Blackie, but his approval didn't extend as far as offering us a discount.

The south-facing garden extends to twelve acres,

and me up, and we made our way from flower bed to flower bed only occasionally encountering other visitors, mostly in the shape of matronly ladies. I felt like a middle-aged Adam in a garden of superannuated Eves, and kept a weather eye out for any incipient signs of serpents in the grass. I thought I'd spotted one when we came upon a goldfish in a pool, as big as any chubb or bream, but it was just, rather like the author, a big fish in a small pond. The far end of the garden was quite a steep climb from the car park, and I couldn't help but admire the determination of some of the older visitors to leave no stone unturned. From the Belvedere at the very furthest and highest corner of the garden a panoramic view extended back over the Staffordshire countryside whose cornfields were busily being harvested. Over a cup of tea, Angela and I looked back over our journey. We had covered fifty-eight miles, quite a respectable total for a day. I felt it had been an eye-opener for Angela, I think she had discovered how comparatively little distance one needs to travel to see new things and fresh perspectives.

'Johnny would have loved this,' she gushed, and I idly wondered if Johnny would thank me if a brave new future stretched before him pottering along the by-roads of Staffordshire. I sincerely hoped so!

Walking Backwards 5

When I boarded the bus and asked for a single to Cheddleton, the friendly driver assumed I was going to see the steam trains, an impression which suggested that I have never quite thrown off the look of a trainspotter acquired in those duffle-bag days of the early 'sixties. When I told him it was the Staffordshire Way I was headed for, he expressed surprise that it even went through Cheddleton. So much for local knowledge!

But it was nice to be travelling independently. Independently, not in the sense that I was alone, but that I was aboard a bus operated by one of the diminishing breed of 'independents', bus companies outside the orbit of the big four national groups. Procters, bless 'em, have been running bus services in North Staffordshire since the 1920s, and though not privy to the politics and economics, I hope they continue to do so for a good deal longer.

He was a chipper little chappy, that driver, indulging in repartee with everyone that boarded his bus.

'You look gorgeous this morning,' he complimented one female passenger.

'You need your eyes testing,' she responded, wearily, 'I've just come off night shift.'

He dropped me off at the bottom of the long hill which slopes down to the canal in Cheddleton.

'I'll wave to you from the top of Mow Cop,' I joked.

'Right mate, I'll look out for that,' my new chum replied, and drove off in a blue haze of diesel fumes, chuckling.

An early morning silence hung over the canal. On a hire boat they were tucking into breakfast, I could just see them through the condensation. A man came past me walking a St Bernard. Alders were perfectly mirrored in the water. To my right the lugubrious tower of St Edwards poked above the tree line.

The Staffordshire Way abandons the Caldon Canal to its own, delightful devices, at Deep Hayes Country Park. Then, in quick succession, it crosses the old Leek to Stoke railway line and the Leek arm of the Caldon Canal. My thoughts turned to *Deli*, and I wondered where Rob was moored now.

It didn't surprise me that several, presumably wealthy people, had chosen to erect substantial houses in this charming neck of the woods. Strolling up Wood Road I admired them each in turn for their eclectic style and the euphonious nature of their names: 'Glenwood', 'The Pines', 'Bracken Cottage' (rather more than a cottage!) 'Delbrook' and 'Fern Glen'. Betjeman would have loved them … they called to mind the Cornish seaside houses so vividly evoked in his poetry.

Beyond the last house the track narrowed and turned north through Hollinhay Wood in which the only audible sound was my breathing, my footfalls, and the distant drone of an aeroplane. Probably it was taking people to America, but why fly to America when you can walk to Leek? It occurred to me that I must have beaten even the dog walkers to the woods that morning, for as I went along my face was breaking spider's webs.

After a while the trees fell away to my right, opening up views of the moorlands beyond Leek. Civilisation returned in a mirror image of the houses at the edge of Hollinhay, another enclave of desirable dwellings, scented gardens and scrupulous lawns: 'The Firs', 'Greenacres', 'Fellside', 'Dragon's Spinney', and – my favourite – a house known simply and plaintively as 'Yonder'; significantly, in some instances the names outsoared the architecture! As I walked past, someone came out of one of the drives in a Jaguar, reinforcing the image of bourgeois contentment.

The Staffordshire Way zigzags over the undulating A53, level with the top of Longsdon church's dumpy spire. I turned right down City Lane – someone's idea of a joke I supposed. A goat offered me a grumbly good morning before I turned a corner and found the church towers and mill chimneys of Leek arranged almost theatrically for my entertainment in the valley below; and beyond, the rocky outline

Rudyard Feeder

of the Country Park, however, the path deteriorated. Running unhedged through open fields, it had been churned up by cattle stooping to quench their thirst in the feeder, I supposed, and there were corridors of reeds and nettles to contend with. The worst thing, where the walker is concerned, about such obstacles, is that so much attention is paid to avoiding being stung or tripped-up, the passing scene is ignored and lost for ever. But life isn't only hard for walkers, on the northernmost hole of the neighbouring golf course, a bunch of golfers were combing the hedgerows for a mislaid ball. A little further on I came upon two blokes in waders painstakingly cutting reeds from the channel. One of them looked up and beseechingly requested the time, as if the Sisyphean task was getting too much for them.

Everyone knows (well don't they?) that a courting couple in the 1860s were so taken with the ambience of Rudyard Lake that they named their first born after it. But a lot less people know that Rudyard Lake is man made, built by the Trent & Mersey Canal Company at the end of the 18th Century to supplement their water supplies: hence the feeder I had been following, for three miles up from the outskirts of Leek. One presumes that Kipling was eternally grateful that his parents didn't do their

of The Roaches. On cue the sun came out, adding clarity and lustre to the view. I descended the edge of a field being grazed by white cattle and then went into the woods which form part of Ladderedge Country Park. A boardwalk carried me across the head of a defile and I wondered if I was far enough north by now for it to be known as a 'clough'.

'This Country Park consists of seventy acres of unimproved grassland, woodland, ponds and streams for you to discover', an interpretive board informed me. I was additionally urged to look out for Speedwell, Knapweed and Yellow Rattle, which sounded like three Shakespearean characters to me. I found myself imagining the area before it had the formality of a country park thrust upon it, picturing it as a resort for millworkers, somewhere they would gravitate to on Sundays, discarding their clogs and shawls for a bit of 'spooning'.

Leek is not officially on the Staffordshire Way, though its fleshpots must tempt all but the most one-eyed of walkers. Cyclopian to a fault (but secretly glad that I had visited it earlier in the book) I followed the official path along the feeder channel which comes down from Rudyard to the Caldon Canal. At first the surface was firm and I scuttled along at a fine pace, pausing only to pat the silky head of a golden retriever called 'Oscar'. Beyond the confines

Reception Committee

Dam Head, Rudyard

courting at Knypersley, another of the canal company's reservoirs.

It was the North Staffordshire Railway who saw the potential for Rudyard as a resort. By then they owned the canal in any case, so it would have seemed wasteful not to develop the area as a mecca for day-trippers and holidaymakers from both their natural catchment area, The Potteries, and further afield. Their railway line from Macclesfield to Uttoxeter ran picturesquely past the eastern side of the lake and they opened a special halt at the top of it as a facility for visitors generally, but golfers specifically, for the railway had cleverly leased out the grounds of Cliffe Park on the opposite side of the water for use as a golf course. Innocent days, innocent pleasures.

There was a good deal of pleasure being had on the shoreline of Rudyard when I arrived, even if the innocence evinced a certain 21st Century world-weariness. In a way it reminded me of Windermere, the same incongruous juxtaposition of funfair and isolation. I dutifully braved the Visitor Centre and learned, amidst other historic trivia, that Blondin twice tight-roped his way across Rudyard, that Captain Webb demonstrated his swimming prowess for the titillation of excited crowds, and that American troops simulated D-Day landings at its northern end. These days folk come to fish, to sail, to canoe, to splash and thrash about in hired rowing boats, and to lick ice cream at the head of the dam. A former

Royal Navy cutter offers trips in season, whilst one and a half miles of the railway (perhaps prematurely abandoned in 1960) have been relaid as a narrow gauge line. On a literary note, it is as a thinly disguised 'Ilam Lake' that Rudyard appears in a short story entitled *The Death of Simon Fuge* by Arnold Bennett.

Trying to find my way northwards from Dam Head, I ended up in a caravan park. I mustn't have been the first, there were a number of hostile notice boards on display, advising walkers to 'get lost'. But the holidaymakers in the caravans and the log cabins were much friendlier, and I got passed down the line – like a ditched pilot in France during the Second World War – under cover of the authorities, until a gate marked 'Private' saw me safely back on to the Staffordshire Way.

Retrospectively, I still can't see where I went wrong, for a fairly broad track traverses the west side of the lake. It provides access to a necklace of waterside properties ranging from cabins to fairly palatial properties. Between them, one gains tantalising glimpses of the lake. I heard a whistle on the wind and looked across to see a little red train chuffling along the opposite shore, the sound of excited children's voices magnified by the mirror-like surface of the water in between. An elderly man emerged from the sailing club with a folder tucked under his arm, a faint smile curled round his lips, I imagined he'd been working on the handicaps for the next weekend's races.

I had gone about a mile along the side of the lake when I came out of some woods and found myself confronted with the Gothic decay of Cliffe Park Hall. The official guide was vague, preferring trees to buildings; alluding to an Irish yew and a wych elm at the expense of the building's history: it took a proper guide book writer to unravel that. Built as a private house after the reservoir had been formed, it had been bought out by the North Staffordshire Railway after a number of years of antagonism between the railway and the owners who objected to the vulgarisation of their view. After the NSR purchased it, it was subsequently employed as a grandiose club house for the golf course. When that was abandoned it became a Youth Hostel and, being more interested in people than trees – well, up to a point – I can tell you that George Orwell dropped by in 1936 on a literary pilgrimage in the wake of Kipling's death. Nowadays it is in private ownership again. There was a quartet of cars parked outside, but it looked as if the occupants would have their work cut out to hold back the house's slow disintegration.

An elderly runner came steadily up the metalled farm track as I was going down it. I offered a few words of encouragement, he didn't appear to need them, but he did wonder if he could get back through to Rudyard village itself the way I'd come. He was running round the lake he explained. I confirmed that he could and watched him continue on his way, hoping that I would be able to run as steadily in a couple of decade's time.

A dark grey cloud came over the rim of the western world, like a bomber looking for a target. At the head of the lake, where it peters out in rushy margins, an old couple were eating bananas. Being thoroughly British we remarked on the cloud, jocularly hoping that it wouldn't see us. The Staffordshire Way adhered itself to the trackbed of the dismantled railway. British Waterways, administrators of Rudyard Lake on behalf of a grateful tax-paying public, had provided facilities for the sort of folk who think the countryside is somewhere to drive out to and park the car in.

I passed beneath the imposing span of a stone-built overbridge, a cousin of the one I had encountered back at Denstone. Then I went over a girder bridge which had carried the railway across a feeder channel which runs into Rudyard from the River Dane to the north-east. I paused for a moment to take in an interesting arrangement of sluice gates and then it began to rain: the bomber pilot may have overlooked me, but his rear-gunner certainly hadn't.

Fortunately I was only half a mile shy of Rushton Spencer where I knew there was a pub alongside the old station. It was a mildly damp and dishevelled rambler who approached the bar at The Knot Inn

Cliffe Park Hall

Rudyard and The Cloud

ten minutes later. To do her justice, the barmaid didn't bat an eyelid, even if some of the more decorously apparelled diners raised their eyebrows. There being no Staffordshire beers on tap, I selected one from nearby Suffolk, and ordered a beef sandwich to accompany it. If the pub was a little over-refurbished for my taste, it certainly knew its business. Service was swift, friendly and efficient. If there was any piped music it was drowned out by its patrons, mostly retired quartets and couples of the sort which fill country pubs at lunchtimes. My sandwich was excellent and while I devoured it I eavesdropped on holidays in Dubrovnik, hormone replacement therapy, and a meandering joke with a chicken as its punchline.

I have driven along the A523 between Leek and Macclesfield on many occasions, but it was more fun to walk unmolested beside it on the old railway. Considering that the line had closed fifty years previously, there seemed to be a lot of ballast underfoot, but I crunched on regardless, as if I was walking across the shingle at Aldeburgh or Dungeness. Then I saw another cloud, well, *The* Cloud really, a millstone grit eminence rising to 1,126 feet above sea level and straddling the boundary between Staffordshire and Cheshire. The comedian(s) who mapped out the Staffordshire Way had deemed it would be fun to lead those who followed in his/their footsteps right to the top and back down again. I had no alternative but to comply.

In the foothills, so to speak, I came upon a trio

The Cloud (Dane Viaduct in the distance)

of ladies picking their way gingerly across a boggy pasture. They were 'doing' the Gritstone Trail, a thirty-five mile hike from Disley, on the outskirts of Stockport, to Kidsgrove. They were taking two and a half days about it, which was fairly respectable going. We walked in single file through a wood, exchanging traveller's tales as though I was doing the Appalachian Trail and they the Sierra Nevadas. But at Raven's Clough – where they politely pointed out that I had turned the wrong way – we tacitly acknowledged that we were marching to the beat of a different drum and they kindly insisted I forge ahead.

The western approach to The Cloud put me in mind of a childhood climb up a Welsh hillside in search of damsons. The gradient was steep but not unduly so. Waymarkers, for once, were plentiful. The only blot on the horizon was another rain cloud. I kept an eye on it trepidatiously. Other corners in my burgeoning view of the landscape were being obliterated by squalls. I felt like a spectator viewing an air raid from a safe distance and thinking: 'they're getting it!'

It got *me* halfway to the top, just as I was crossing the by-road which leads to the aptly christened hamlet of Cloud Side. Reaching for my mobile, I sent a text to a friend to tell them that I had verification that clouds consist of water. Once I'd crossed the road, gaining the summit seemed a formality. The visible

Climbing up to The Cloud

world had divided itself in two; one half shrouded in mist and rain, the other beaming sunnily. It was a metaphor for existence. I trudged up to the trig point, sodden. The toposcope, which normally would have entranced me for hours, was given the cold shoulder. Of the way off The Cloud there was literally no sign. I risked getting the map out of my rucksack, even if thirty seconds of exposure to the rain would reduce it to pulp. It did not help that my glasses were steamed up. It did not help that I realised I was in Cheshire!

Retrospectively, I'm convinced I served the purpose of drying out The Cloud. Certainly I carried large amounts of its moisture away with me.

Timbersbrook

My shorts could not have been wetter if I'd swum out to sea in them. My spirits could not have been damper if Arsenal had lost to a controversial penalty in injury time. The descent on the Cheshire side of The Cloud, through bracken and over rocks, seemed interminable, even though the sunshine was hastening up to meet me, wafting golden rays in the general direction of its prodigal son. Gritstone Trail signs had supplanted Staffordshire Way waymarkers like an invasive plant, but I was still too wet to care. It hardly registered that the fields around Timbersbrook were as sodden as I was. In the fullness of time I reached sanctuary in the shape of the Biddulph Valley Way, the well-surfaced trackbed of a former branch of the North Staffordshire Railway. This I followed until Staffordshire was regained at Whitemoor, noting that, behind me, the 'Welcome to Cheshire' sign was rather more elaborate than the 'Welcome to Staffordshire' one in front. How many sub-committee meetings had it taken to decide on the budget for the respective signage?

After a couple of miles I left the old railway and climbed the lane towards Higher Whitemoor Farm. It was easy to put oneself in the place of past generations, rolling jubilantly back in the family Land Rover from a successful day at the fat stock sales. But it was just as facile to picture trying to forge a path

through snowdrifts when the bank manager had refused to extend the overdraft.

'Eggs for Sale' said the sign on the gateway – I didn't need eggs, I needed homemade ginger beer!

Now it was bright and warm in the wake of the rain, and The Cloud looked as though butter wouldn't melt in its farmhouse-baked mouth. In the wood it was cooler. I minced over exposed roots. I squelched through peaty pools. A jay took the mickey out of me. I was a soft target.

When the woods receded, I found myself on another farm track. To the east Biddulph was spreading out of the folds of its valley like an obese teenager. I arrived at a point marked on the map as Nick i' th' Hill. One side of the path appeared to be in Staffordshire, the other in Cheshire, I was playing hopscotch with the counties. A blonde with two pit bulls came past me, bidding hello in what Ray Davies once called 'a dark brown voice'; deep vocal chords these North Staffs lasses.

The penultimate mile of my Staffordshire Way trek lay over a ludicrously busy by-road. Everyone, it appeared, was intent on driving to the top of the escarpment for a better view. I came upon a toposcope erected by the Rotary Club of Biddulph in 1980 to mark the 75th anniversary of Rotary International. There was no quibbling with the panorama it presented. I could make out The Wrekin, the Breiddens, Beeston Tor, the Welsh Hills, Helsby Hill, and … the soap works at Warrington. The lay-by was knee-deep in litter, and gave every indication of being used as Congleton's closest approximation to the mile high club.

'There is nothing at the end of any road better than can be found along it' – the wisdom of Edward Thomas was foremost in my mind as I approached Mow Cop, ninety-two miles, not counting the detours and diversions, from Kinver Edge. It was a land of small holdings, folk who did a bit of farming and a bit of dealing in scrap, and kept their heads below the radar of the revenue. Never having put much faith in uniformity, I warm to such ambivalences. I was too tired, and too residually damp, to pay too much attention to the Old Man of Mow, a pillar of rock absentmindedly left behind by quarrying. I walked on to Mow Cop Castle, a folly, or 'eye-catcher', erected in 1754 to romanticise the view from Rode Hall down on the Cheshire Plain. Quite a number of people had walked from as far away as the car park to have their photograph taken beside it.

Perching myself on a rock, I relived my journey, fast-forwarding it like that old film they used to show you of the Brighton Belle. When I reached Ladderedge Park I pressed 'pause', and stopped to re-read an interpretive board: 'Did I know that walking for thirty minutes, five times a week could significantly improve my health, reduce weight and blood pressure, risk of heart disease, diabetes, stress, and make me feel happier and more energised?'

'What about seven hours a day, five times a week?' I called out loud, to the amazement of passers-by,' would that not make me immortal?'

Mow Cop

Index

Acknowledgements

The author fervently wishes his credentials could be enhanced by a lengthy list of contributors, associates and experts, but the fact is, the contents are largely his own; rare insights and glaring omissions alike. He did, however, receive much valued assistance in the facilitation of his journeys from Angela Johnson and Rob Cooper, the accommodating owners of *Blackie* and *Deli* respectively.

Either side of being hospitalised, Karen Tanguy gamely provided transport, editing expertise and additional photography, namely the pictures on pages 17, 25, 80, 107 upper left & lower, 108 lower, 112, 113 & 140.

The management and staff at Hawksworth of Uttoxeter could not have been more encouraging or supportive in the preparation of this book, but special thanks must go to Simon Hawksworth who bore the time-consuming and will-sapping brunt of the author's stubbornly film-based photography and esoteric software.

Thanks are due to the people who unwittingly made cameo appearances within these pages. The author trusts they do not feel themselves misrepresented, and that they appreciate that any fun being poked is of the most gentle variety.

Finally the author's family deserve appreciation for generously tolerating his frequent bouts of truancy, lamely excused as 'work'.

The Author

Michael Pearson is a chronicler of place, as exemplified by the *Canal Companion* series of guide books he has been producing for nearly thirty years. He writes also of railway matters, and his travels by this mode of transport have taken him from Penzance to Thurso and Arisaig to Lowestoft: the most southerly, northerly, westerly and easterly stations in Britain respectively. Many of his passions – such as beer drinking and pie eating – have been seamlessly absorbed into his work, but he finds occasional release in long distance running and the quixotic scorelines of his favourite football teams: Arsenal, Queen of the South and Carmarthen Town.